"Brad Federman has created a practical, systematic, real world guide for leaders of all sizes and types of organizations to truly engage individuals and teams. *Employee Engagement* will not only convince any leader, from the CEO of the largest company to the owner of the smallest of small businesses that engaged team members lead to efficient, profitable and successful organizations, but it will also give them the tools to make engagement happen."

Rick McCue vice president,
Brand Performance & Support Embassy Suites Hotels

"Brad Federman's new book is a must read! It provides the critical keys for performance improvement and employee engagement in the context of our ever-changing global landscape. It teaches how to embrace technology overload without violating the sanctity of high-trust, engaged relationships. For improved business principles resulting in more profit, read this book!"

Don Hutson, co-author of NY Times #1 best-seller,
The One Minute Entrepreneur, and CEO of U. S. Learning

"Brad Federman offers new insight on the difference between employee satisfaction and employee engagement. Any manager, business owner or HR professional who wants to be successful in today's world will benefit from his perspective on the importance of employee engagement in reducing turnover, building customer loyalty, increasing profits and sustaining a corporate culture built on integrity and trust."

Rose Douglass, SPHR executive vice president
director of human resources Central Bank

"I have worked with Brad firsthand to transform our company's sales culture. This book captures the insights of his expertise and is a must read for driving your business to the next level."

John Ray president and CEO TopRX, Inc.

"Nearly 90 years of evolutionary thinking on engagement in one resource. This is the roadmap to engagement and excellence!"

Bob Chamness EVP, CLO & secretary Digimarc Corporation

"Like great architecture, Brad has clearly laid out a solid foundation that's built to last the test of time. Following his differentiating blueprint of connecting employee's needs to a company's goals will positively transform people's lives both in and outside the office walls."

Courtney Rothstein executive vice president,
managing director Added Value

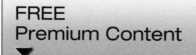

FREE
Premium Content

JOSSEY-BASS™
An Imprint of
WILEY

This book includes premium content that can be accessed from our Web site when you register at **www.Josseybass.com/go/bradfederman** using the password ***professional***.

For my wife, Hollie, who has always believed in me, and our boys, Aris and Elijah, who help me make believe.

Employee Engagement

A Roadmap for Creating Profits, Optimizing Performance, and Increasing Loyalty

Brad Federman

JOSSEY-BASS
A Wiley Imprint
www.josseybass.com

Published by Jossey-Bass
A Wiley Imprint
989 Market Street, San Francisco, CA 94103-1741—www.josseybass.com

Jossey-Bass books and products are available through most bookstores. To contact Jossey-Bass directly call our Customer Care Department within the U.S. at 800-956-7739, outside the U.S. at 317-572-3986, or fax 317-572-4002.

Jossey-Bass also publishes its books in a variety of electronic formats. Some content that appears in print may not be available in electronic books.

Library of Congress Cataloging-in-Publication Data
Federman, Brad.
　　Employee engagement: a roadmap for creating profits, optimizing performance, and increasing loyalty / Brad Federman.-1st ed.
　　　　p.　cm.
　　Includes bibliogrpahical references and index.
　　ISBN 978-0-470-38815-0 (cloth)
　　　1. Employee motivation.　2. Management—Employeee participation.　3. Employees—Attitudes.　I. Title.
　　HF5549.5.M63F43　2009
　　658.3'14—dc22
　　　　　　　　　　　　　　　　　　　　　　　　　　　　2009017416

Printed in the United States of America
FIRST EDITION
HB Printing　　　　10 9 8 7 6 5 4 3 2 1
PB Printing　　　　10 9 8 7 6 5 4 3 2 1

Contents

Foreword

Tom Schmitt

President and Chief Executive Officer, FedEx Global Supply Chain Services

Brad Federman has spent most of his life with an eye toward strategy, execution, and performance. In fact, as early as junior high he showed an inherent knack for suggesting ways to improve group performance. His abilities surfaced during a weekend retreat and leadership seminar for student government participants, when the camp director immediately recognized in Brad a keen understanding of people and the issues that make them what they are.

Brad is now widely recognized as an expert in performance improvement and as a coach and leader. He has now made the decision to share that knowledge on a broader scale, and I predict that this book will be seen on quite a few executive bookshelves.

Managing people in a corporate setting shouldn't be rocket science. After all, it requires only hiring qualified people, keeping them reasonably happy with pleasant working conditions and salaries, and motivating them to perform well and help the company make a profit. Not too hard, right? Right!—As long as "managing people" is the end goal.

Brad is on the leading edge of an area that has been evolving ever since Frederick Taylor first turned management into a science in the early 1900s. It was only then that businesses got the first inkling that their way of getting the product out the door might be more than a little inefficient.

The business community has come even further since Taylor's day, taking a more holistic look at leadership. We now look for traits such as emotional intelligence—the ability to assess and manage our own emotions as well as those of others. Leadership is finally being seen as a quality instead of an authority. Good managers are not judged by how well they keep a team in line and how much work that team produces, but rather by how good they are at motivating a team to want to produce a better product. We're looking deeper at employees to learn just what makes them tick—and, thereby, learning what makes them work. Left-brain people learn and process information much differently than right-brain people. Choose all of one type and your team will suffer. Choose a balance of left and right and you'll have drive, strategy, and creativity.

Brad puts the icing on the cake with his in-depth look at employee engagement as a strategy. He compares his model to Herzberg's "Two Factor" model. It is some of that and a little of the old adage about "leading a horse to water." You can put an employee in a spacious office with an inspiring view, but without what Brad calls the "enrichment" factor, you cannot force him to be motivated or to care deeply about the company's goals.

With rock-solid advice on everything from employee surveys to hiring the right people, this book will live up to its claim as a "roadmap for creating profits, optimizing performance, and increasing loyalty."

Preface

In March 2003, my life changed. I was no longer working with my old company. After almost nine years, we parted ways. It was a difficult time for me because many of my colleagues were like family. On the other hand, I watched and was asked to participate in some of the poorest people practices I had seen in a while. I saw relationships deteriorate and performance fall as a result. Ironically, I was working for a performance improvement firm at the time and it was clear that the new owners chose "profit" over "people." I had always been involved in the performance improvement world, but my interests were now different. I needed to reconnect with my chosen field and I found myself asking, "How can I feel that sense of commitment again?"

Significant and widespread changes had occurred in the previous two to three years. First, the Internet bubble burst, and many people saw their life savings spill away. After that came the tragic events of 9/11. Meanwhile, globalization continued at a rapid pace.

The world has become smaller and our interdependency as a global community has become more apparent. What has also become apparent is our common struggle as human beings for respect, trust, understanding, and a desire to live and work productively.

In the Middle East, I saw many employees at an organization with which I was working wanting to move past organizational and cultural confines that were no longer productive. They wanted to be more engaged at work and stand for something inspiring and of value, and yet on a day-to-day basis they needed the basics. Unfortunately, as in many organizations, they felt as though their hands were tied. And as I traveled the globe, I saw the same phenomenon repeat itself again and again.

I began to ask myself why work felt this way for so many people. With all of the training and interventions available, why was the environment of so many companies so far from stellar? And besides feeling good, did it really matter? Maybe "people" and "profits" were not as connected as I had thought. With those questions in mind, I began to rethink my past thirteen years in the industry, and I came to a few key realizations:

- Many of the interventions in the workplace are based on old research that reflects a different time;
- Organizations do not deal with key issues, such as "building trust" and "working through fear," in much of our training;
- Our tendency is to make "or" decisions versus "and" decisions, causing us to function in an exclusive versus inclusive manner; and
- Our ability to truly link "people" to "profit" still had a way to go.

This book is the result of those realizations. It is an overview of the employee engagement realm. Each chapter could be a book in and of itself. My attempt is to provide a strong overview of the subject with practical ideas that will cause people to think and a roadmap to a more productive future.

In the end, I have tried to provide both a C-level perspective and a human resource perspective, as I do not see them as an "or" proposition. My hope is that this book will help raise the human element of the business to the boardroom, because those who follow the advice in this book will create workplaces with more committed employees rather than compliant ones, more meaningful environments rather than insignificant ones, build stronger relationships with their employees, and outperform their competition.

Acknowledgments

This book is a synthesis of many ideas that come from various places, including theory, application, and experience specific to employee engagement and interrelated topics such as psychology and adult learning. Employee engagement is the integration of motivation, performance, and business. I have found exploring this aspect of organizational life insightful and valuable. I know that this book would never have been possible without the help and support of many people along the way.

I wish to thank, first and foremost, my clients who have helped to build the bridge between organizational need and organizational life. I have been lucky to work with people who do not want to settle for what is, but who want to work for what could be. My clients are an inspiration to me, and they have allowed me both the space and freedom to be creative and the proximity to be a partner in addressing their needs. I also wish to thank colleagues who helped me along the way and from whom I've learned so much. Melissa Booth, your help proofreading and editing my work is not forgotten. You have a unique ability to think about the readers and see things from their perspective. Sean Murray, you have been a great person to work with and have always added value to my thinking. Neal Nadler, I am grateful I went to Vanderbilt; otherwise, I would not have met you. Your teaching and advice have helped shape my career. Thank you, also, to all of my colleagues who have helped and encouraged me along the way.

There are key moments in a person's life when individuals have an opportunity to make a difference. I want to thank two mentors who made a difference in my life, Mike Michaelson and Dru Bagwell.

Last, I wish to thank the publishing team at John Wiley & Sons, and everyone who contributed to the production of this book. I know how hard you worked.

Introduction

By selecting this book, you have made an investment of your time and resources. You should expect to receive information you can apply directly to the needs of your organization and its employees.

The content on the following pages is designed to provide the information you are seeking. By maximizing your own level of engagement as you read the book, you will maximize the book's benefit to you. Therefore, I encourage you to think about your organization and your role in that organization as you move through this book. Questions to ask yourself include:

- What vision, goals, and expectations am I trying to meet, both personally and professionally?
- What level of engagement will this require?
- What is the current level of engagement within my organization, and what pain or obstacles am I encountering on the road to a more engaged, fun, and profitable organization?
- How important is loyalty to this equation?

This book, and the resources and expertise behind it, will help you answer these questions. More importantly, they will help you bring the vision of a more engaged organization to reality.

I encourage you to begin by writing brief notes in response to the questions above. As you move through the chapters, add to these notes, creating your own framework and outline for engagement as you go. You may wish to share this information, and your response to it, with other members of your organization as you explore and address these issues together.

The text provides a current, practical, and comprehensive view of the issues of engagement. It is written to be read from start to finish to best understand and contextualize the information presented. However, you will find that the individual chapters can also be used as stand-alone "tutorials," as they contain insights and questions you can apply to specific issues.

By approaching this book and the issues of engagement with specific goals in mind, you will not only have a roadmap to profits, performance, and loyalty, but you will have begun the journey to the results you are seeking.

Remember, the value of this information is in its application—knowing what engagement looks and feels like in your organization and— based on that knowledge—building a culture of trust and achievement. The path is clear, and the rewards are significant. Proven guidelines, tools, and resources are waiting to assist you.

In the following pages, you will find validation of your commitment to excellence; the experience and insights of numerous leaders who chose the path you are taking; and the wisdom of my organization and others who have had the opportunity to counsel and assist these courageous leaders in pursuing even greater levels of achievement.

I hope you will gain as much from reading the book as I have gained from the relationships and experiences that led me to write it.

Section One

ENGAGEMENT FOUNDATIONS

1

THE CASE FOR EMPLOYEE ENGAGEMENT: CONNECTIONS VERSUS TRANSACTIONS

For a while now, the employer/employee relationship has been deteriorating. Some might even say that this relationship no longer exists. Currently, studies estimate that only 11 to 29 percent of employees are fully engaged in their work.[1,2] See Figure 1.1 for a typical engagement spectrum.

What we find when we look at a typical distribution of employees across the employee engagement spectrum is that our organizations are being driven forward by a select few. The bar graph in Figure 1.1 reflects the actual distribution of one of

Figure 1.1 Typical Employee Engagement Distribution

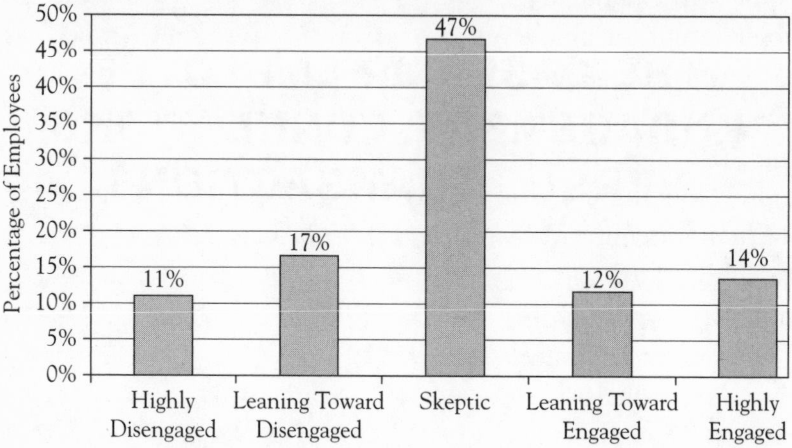

Source: Performancepoint, LLC

our clients and it is not atypical. Our organizations tend to look like a bell curve, with only a small fraction of employees clearly connected to their work and the strategy of the organization. Think about this for a moment. Would we settle for these types of numbers in any other area of our business? Would you be willing to have only 14 percent of your systems, copy machines, printers, or facilities functioning at full capacity? The answer is obviously "no." When we lose capacity in any other part of our business, we invest or reinvest—and we should do the same with our people.

We are challenged to locate qualified associates to meet the competitive standards of today's work environment. It is a struggle to find great employees, let alone keep them, even with only 3.6 million open positions in the United States alone.[3] When the economy falters, and we have an easier time hiring qualified employees because there are more candidates available, we do not hire and on-board them well. In a recent survey completed by Performancepoint, over 42 percent of respondents claimed finding qualified employees as one of their biggest challenges, yet only slightly over 10 percent of them claimed that their organizations excelled at selecting and on-boarding new employees.[4]

Even when we hire great employees, the complexities that come with managing today's diverse workforce can create difficult retention challenges. In the board room, executives talk about the new generation lacking in a work ethic and the desire of some employees to move up in the organization without paying their dues. To compensate, companies spend a great deal of money looking into the implications of generational differences in their organizations, sometimes forgetting that, while these generalizations can be productively made across larger populations, they cause problems when applied on an individual level.

We must remember that each employee is an individual, and these individuals do not necessarily conform to generalizations. A great example is the contrast between many baby boomers I have met who are tech-savvy and some of the young people entering the workforce who are not. It is even more ironic that some of my client contacts in human resources, charged with improving the current engagement situation at their company, have confided in me that they want to leave and don't feel engaged themselves—a strong signal of the current state of affairs.

On the other side, employees are tired of being taken for granted. They do not feel respected and included. Many employees want more transparency and question senior leadership's choices. Young, old, male, female; it does not really matter; everyone wants to feel more connected. But we have grown to lack trust in our organizations. Performancepoint notes that only 28 percent of employees truly believe in the strategic direction of their organizations and just over 38 percent trust their leadership.[5] We have either been laid off ourselves or know someone who has or we have been asked to be a good corporate citizen, only to watch as some of our fellow citizens are mistreated.

Engagement Factors

How did we get to this point? Will it pass? Or are we condemned to this new world where "everyone is in it for themselves" and it is just too hard to move forward with this drag?

Figure 1.2 Macro Shifts in the Employment Environment

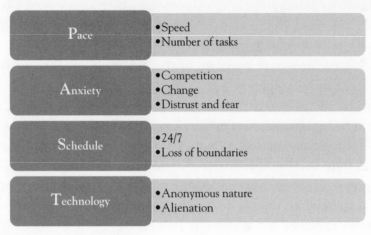

Source: Performancepoint, LLC

Well, the bad news is that these challenges are not going to go away. The good news is that there are a number of ways to work within this new context. Companies that have figured this out typically experience a significant "leg up" when it comes to the numbers. But that is not the only benefit. To understand how we can work productively in this environment, we need to look at why these changes have occurred. See Figure 1.2 for a number of macro shifts that have caused these changes.

Pace

Everything is happening faster than ever. It is difficult for organizations and individuals to keep up. Many of us are frantic and under pressure on a daily basis. In the last forty years, we have moved from typewriters and land lines to laptops and cell phones. We used to have conversations in the office anticipating the ideal environment technology would bring. Now most of us can be overheard asking questions like, "Do our computers work for us or do we work for our computers?" The truth is that technology has created two fundamental shifts in our work pace:

- We can process more information faster.
- It is no longer necessary for us to be present when certain work is taking place.

While this sounds great in theory, we are not any faster ourselves as human beings, and now we are straddled with the demand to keep up with more information, more data, and higher expectations of productivity. Specifically, the speed of our work has increased and the number of tasks we must accomplish in a given time period has increased as well. With all of this new capability, we feel the increased demands made by our organizations, leadership, and customers. One study in Europe that was completed over a fifteen-year period found a trend that more workers are experiencing a higher pace of work with an increase in the amount of tight deadlines.[6] These rising expectations cause us to focus on the "little picture" rather than the "big picture."

In one of our training exercises, we ask participants to achieve a basic goal. We even allow them time to plan how they will approach the task. However, they rarely achieve the goal because they jump right into the task rather than planning, due to their perceived time deadline. Participants focus on the little details and tasks that they can quickly impact, and they just try to get the work done. Interestingly enough, when we review the task at a more strategic level, they quickly realize what high performance could look like and begin to explore why they did not even see the more powerful and productive approach.

When we arrive at work and we have fifty, one hundred . . . some clients complain to me that they have over two hundred or more emails in their inboxes at the start of the day, without being out of the office on the previous day . . . and we have several projects with which we are involved, and a supervisor who has just informed us of a new deadline, we have a difficult time not getting caught up in that noise. All of us become distracted and overwhelmed at times. We find ourselves asking, "How can I get through all of this quickly?" or "What can I check off the list?" In many cases, we give up a strategic point of view just to complete more tasks, faster. Yes, we are productive, but are we always making a difference? Are we engaged in the right tasks? Are we driving the organization forward?

A great example of this is the numerous requests my organization receives regarding team building. Most of these requests involve one person or a team complaining about another person or team not involving them in their efforts. The paradox is that the other person or team feels like they cannot collaborate due to the time it takes, and they feel damned if they do, and damned if they don't. So the question becomes whether it is best to work strategically, involving others and leaving less time to complete tasks in a quality manner, or to get more things done in a less-collaborative manner.

One critical aspect of our work that suffers because of this overload is our relationships. We lack the time to take interest in others, and we certainly have a challenge exploring issues that are important to other people, including our employees. After all, these conversations feel like distractions from getting more tasks completed, faster. The implication is that this pace has caused many of us to focus on efficiency and treat even our relationships as transactional. Many managers cannot tell you what their employees' career goals are or how their employees prefer to be recognized. Why? The number-one reason I hear from managers is, "I don't have the time." They don't feel they have the time, and yet the definition of being a manager is all about making the time for your employees.

When I talk with employees, I am amazed at how much pressure they feel. I am even more amazed when they talk about how little they feel appreciated in comparison. These employees do not think about moving the business forward, how to reduce the pressure, or change the environment (although that is a wish). These employees ask themselves: "Is this worth it?" or "Where else can I work?"

Anxiety

The pace of work alone gives credence to the fact that many people feel a significant amount of stress and anxiety, but that is not the only cause of anxiety in the workplace. The pressure to perform is significant. First and foremost, I can think of very few businesses that are not under pressure from *increased competition*. I know many of our clients struggle with increased costs, pricing pressures, and shrinking profits. Much of this competition is due to globalism, trade agreements, and technology.[7] It is amazing how much work is completed across borders.

I travel a great deal to Europe and the Middle East for clients whose engagement and productivity demands have increased as these boundaries have diminished. Most people outside the Middle East region would not recognize the changes creating increased demand to engage employees in that workplace. First of all, many people are not aware of the economies that are being built outside of the oil industry. And the majority of individuals are not aware of the region's challenges in building engagement of locals, or "nationals" as is the case in Kuwait, where the engagement of expatriates is higher than that of locals. This creates challenges related to employment, immigration, efficiencies, and economic stability.[8]

Technology has not only allowed us to service customers globally, but it has opened up markets to competition they have not experienced before. This forces businesses operating in these markets to be more competitive. There are many things that a business cannot easily change, such as the environmental or employment regulations of a particular country. Many businesses work instead on innovation or increasing efficiencies. Other corporations focus on off-shoring, use of expatriates, and leveraging contract workers. Regardless of the strategy, movement across borders, individual assignments, and increased job competition leave individuals with a "Me" attitude. Why shouldn't they feel that way? These employees want to make their marks and make as much money as they can when they can. Who knows what tomorrow will bring?

Another area that creates anxiety is *change*. We are constantly asked to do things differently than we have in the past. Part of this phenomenon has to do with the increased pace in our workplaces. Another aspect has to do with the lack of consistency in leadership. With the median CEO tenure of 5.5 years[9] and turnover of CEOs at its highest rate ever over the last two years,[10] we barely have enough time to execute one strategy before another one is being introduced. One of our clients had six CEOs in four years. Every time a new CEO walked in their door, employees were asked to buy into a different strategy. Talk about whiplash.

The last area that contributes to anxiety is all about *security and trust*. Layoffs have become commonplace. Ethics and integrity seem optional until someone has to pay the piper, as in the case of Enron. Choices made by boards of directors or executives based on greed, as well as inequities in compensation systems, make many employees feel slighted at best. It is startling how many times I work with people who quit a company only to return six months later in order to be paid more. How can we have compensation systems that ignore productive, knowledgeable employees and reward unproven workers who present a learning curve and increased risk?

Another area that has come under fire in recent years is *executive pay*. There are a number of recent examples of executives receiving bonuses when their companies have been losing money and laying off workers. In the United States, we have seen this debate occur even when companies have received bailout money from the government. Jack Welch has even weighed in on the debate saying:

> "I think without question once the federal government has to step in to bail out the private enterprise, you've got to modify the private enterprise pay packages."[11]

The point is not about whether or not executive pay is fair, which of course is situational. The point is about trust. Consider another headline "Where Bribery Was Just a Line Item,"[12] referring to Siemens business practices, or "The Party's Over"[13] quoting Attorney General of New York Andrew Cuomo on AIG's over-the-top executive expenditures.

Are we running organizations in a transparent manner, communicating well enough with all of our stakeholders, with clear reasonable choices? Perception is powerful. When we lose sight of how our employees, our customers, and the general public perceive our actions, we have created a significant problem. When pressure overrides good judgment and forces unhealthy choices, we all pay.

Risk also takes on new proportions in the *global marketplace*. A war in Lebanon starts and everyone evacuates. Hugo Chavez threatens to seize control of private business, some of which is owned and operated by companies outside of Venezuela. Rebuilding Iraq remains a pressing agenda in a conflict-ridden region. We take risks doing business globally every day.

The more unstable the world becomes, the more reactionary many of us become. Organizations hedge their bets. Some organizations lack necessary disaster recovery plans. These organizations become driven by short-term thinking because the opportunity exists now. We live with more fear and uncertainty, which limits trust and increases insecurity.

Each time I go to the Middle East, I am curious about the differences between cultures—business and personal. One of the interesting things I have noted in my travels there is the ability of individuals to cope with conflict and uncertainty from day to day. Some of these wonderful people travel to neighboring countries where I would not dream to go. I would not put my life at that much risk. However, I also note that many of these same people seem to lack trust in others and lack a sense of security in their work environment, so they find security in themselves. Fear causes us to go inward. Fear causes us to take fewer risks, and when we do take them, the risks are based on fear, not opportunity. Unfortunately, this has become a major issue in our workplaces.

According to the Human Resources Workplace Stress Survey completed in 2007[14]:

- Seventy percent of HR professionals feel stress is a problem in their organization;
- Over 50 percent believe stress has become a larger issue in just one year; and
- Only 10 percent of line managers are aware, to a great extent, of what signs to look for to identify stress.

Many of the solutions the research pointed to were reactive. Organizations sometimes utilize workplace stress policies as a solution to the problem. Other organizations utilize employee assistance programs (EAPs), which are reactive in nature and usually come into effect when the problem looms large. As a whole, we are behind in our efforts to provide the skills necessary to keep up with the anxiety and stress in today's workplace.

Schedule

Because we are working across the globe, business truly is twenty-four hours, seven days a week for many organizations. That type of effort creates interesting lifestyles for employees of those organizations. Many of these individuals are facing constant jet lag from traveling to places like China one week, and then to the United States the very next. Even if we are not one of those individuals who must fly to the ends of the earth, we are wired. Most people have PDAs and can be reached wherever they are. More importantly, we have become dependent on these devices, even addicted. Our boundaries have all but disappeared.

The larger concern regarding this stressful workplace revolves around expectations and balance. When does work stop? How do I find balance? What if not taking a call costs the organization money? If I do not work at odd times, will I be left out of the loop? What impact will that have on my career? The fact that these questions are on employees' minds tells us a great deal. Many employees suffer from a struggle with work/life balance.

I, myself, could work all of the time. I know I can't find balance; I can only work toward it. It has become a process composed of choices, not an outcome. This is like having an additional responsibility that comes along with work. If we do not pay attention to ourselves, it usually leads to burnout. And if we try to unplug when others around us do not, other stresses may result.

The results of the 24/7 workplace can be quite traumatic. Many negative results occur because of this lifestyle, including sleep disorders, health problems, parenting challenges, marital discord, household chore difficulties, and minimized family time. It has been argued that this issue needs to become a publicly debated topic and that social and business reforms are necessary in order to support the expansion of the 24/7 work environment.[15] Regardless of whether there are policy changes or not, one thing is certain: employees have new challenges due to a global schedule and demand that has both positive and negative consequences, blurring the line even more between personal and professional life.

Technology

It is interesting that all of this technology has not made our corporate or personal lives easier. Businesses struggle because they hire professionals; many highly educated, and then put these associates into boxes. We call these boxes, collectively, an organizational chart. Then we put in place *limits* known as policies. The more we try to regulate our employees, the more we create a parent-child relationship. Our employees feel as though they are wearing shackles. I worked with one company that made all employees submit a purchase order for approval on everything regardless of the amount or purpose. Needless to say, the organization had a backlog on approvals, sometimes up to two months. They had service technicians in the field who had to make a choice—buy a part using their own money and risk not being reimbursed, or choose to make the customer wait for an unacceptable amount of time. A number of these service technicians chose to forgo reimbursement in order to service customers. They did not submit reimbursement forms because they were afraid of the potential repercussions.

Our organizational charts are based on the demands of the industrial age and a traditional military structure or hierarchy. This structure was created for a time when we did not use computers, networks, PDAs, and other Internet-based technologies. Most employees were hired to function as labor—and not highly skilled labor at that.

To compensate for this discrepancy, organizations have utilized or experimented with various structures such as the matrix organization and skunk works. There have been some limited successes, but overall we are still struggling. Corporate structures are shifting, and they should continue this shift in keeping with the new work environment. Until we create a new, more adaptable and accepted model, we can expect continuing sub-optimization of talent and resources, creation of conflict, or worse.

At a conference at which I recently spoke, a discussion developed around this very topic. Some people attending the conference spoke of their employers' policies limiting use of social networks such as LinkedIn. There was clearly frustration with policies limiting the use of the Internet, new technologies, and structures that function more like a network than a traditional hierarchy. Of course, organizations that support these types of shifts will lose a sense of control, but what might they gain?

Jeff Howe in *CrowdSourcing*[16] shares numerous examples of organizations large and small that have utilized these new structures and technologies to improve products, the customer interface, and their business. He relates some key principles behind why *CrowdSourcing* is successful:

- Communities can organize labor more effectively than organizations;
- The most appropriate person to complete the work is the one who is passionate about the work; not necessarily the person with the job title;
- Evaluation is most helpful and productive when coming from peers; and
- When work is organized through these types of networks, people join in eagerly to help out their friends or collegial peers.

To a lot of people this will sound like anarchy. What about going through the proper structure or channels? What about the rules? How can you bypass your boss or supervisor? How can we include outsiders (people not in the company) in these projects? What about copyrights, patents, confidential information? How can we protect ourselves? This is too risky. Or is it too risky not to figure out a way to make new structures work? Think about Procter and Gamble, the Linux operating system, open source programming, or Wikis. Each of these is an example of an organization or project that has benefited from these new structures and ways of working. It is happening right now, whether we like it or not. The question is how we can use it to our advantage and engage our people more.

The current environment also encourages employees to multi-task, which might be appropriate when we keep in mind the second half of that word—TASK. Unfortunately, we as a society also include people in multi-tasking. All this does is allow us to treat each other superficially, as if we were on a checklist. The consequence of this is interruption and isolation. Many employees utilize email and text messaging as a replacement for dialogue. We even see email utilized as a vehicle for airing our conflicts. Consider the impact on our relationships when we do not have to look the other person in the eye or hear his or her voice, and all we have to do to conclude our dialogue is to press "send" or "delete." One manager with whom I was working had two cell phones, a computer, and a land line. He would talk with one person, keep another person on hold, check email on the other line, and answer the phone on the desk. How do you think his employees felt? Unfortunately, I know how he felt—productive.

The average number of minutes employees have to focus on a project prior to being interrupted is eleven minutes.[17] Think about the time it takes to shift your thinking and then to shift back to the project; to review and figure out where you left off. How much aggravation do we develop over interruptions? Or if you are the one waiting . . . how do you feel? We have all become too comfortable with instant gratification. We want answers quickly, and unfortunately life does not usually work that way. More importantly, the recent trend toward multi-tasking actually slows us down and limits our focus. Kathleen Nadeau, Ph.D., says, "Multi-tasking is really a misnomer, since your brain is unable to focus on two tasks at once." And another expert, Rene Marois, Ph.D., explains why we are less efficient based on research she has completed, "A kind of bottleneck occurs and you become less efficient than if you were to finish one task before starting another."[18] The ramifications are huge. We are slower, yet we have the opposite perception; we are not present and available for our colleagues, yet we feel we are meeting everyone's needs.

As productive as we may think we are, we are not there for each other. We are alone even when we are with people. We feel like a bother to others or are frustrated with those who try to treat us like just another task. It is easier to isolate ourselves and hide behind text messages and emails.

In the last several years, we have seen increased job competition and movement. We used to take assignments as a development rotation. Many people now must take positions on a contract basis or across the globe, due to the new nature of work. While exciting, this dynamic creates a transient work population. Teams have difficulty forming; we can begin to have a loss of institutional or department memory; relationships only develop to a limited degree; and people do not have to live with the consequences of their decisions because they have left before those consequences materialize.

All these forces lead us to be transactional and efficient. To hide inside ourselves. However, high-quality human relationships are much more consultative and collaborative. They are based on trust and value. We work with people and organizations in which we have faith, and that help us become successful and better than we are when we work individually. Those organizations that build processes, systems, and relationships based on these principles are winning in the marketplace. See Figure 1.3, The Current Dichotomy.

What do we mean by winning? Lower turnover, higher productivity, stronger customer loyalty, and a better bottom line.

Figure 1.3 The Current Dichotomy

Current Forces
Transactional
Efficient
Superficial

Needed Efforts
Consultative
Collaborative
Supportive

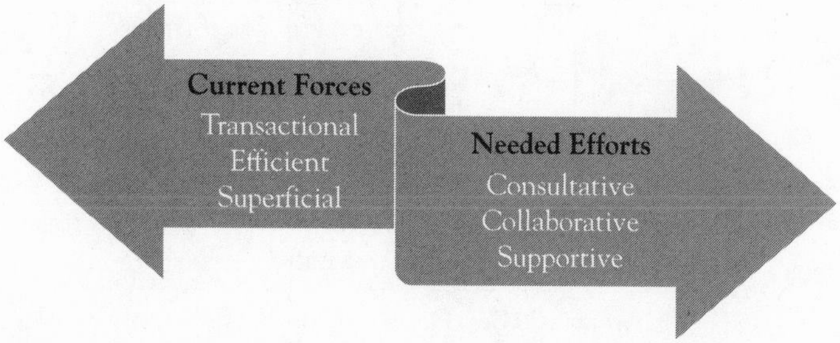

Source: Performancepoint, LLC

Turnover

We would all like to have more control over the turnover rates in our organizations. This is not to say we want to eliminate turnover altogether. After all, some turnover is productive and has a positive impact for individuals and organizations. However, in my work, I rarely come across companies keeping every associate they want to keep and removing those they do not want to keep. More times than not, organizations would like to reduce the amount of turnover they are experiencing. Interestingly enough, turnover and engagement are interrelated.

Take for instance, the Fortune 100 Best Places to Work[19] list, which are considered companies with high employee engagement levels. The turnover rates for these organizations are much lower than the industry average, sometimes by as much as 71 percent, as in the case of the healthcare industry.[20] See Figure 1.4 on the relationship between engagement and turnover.

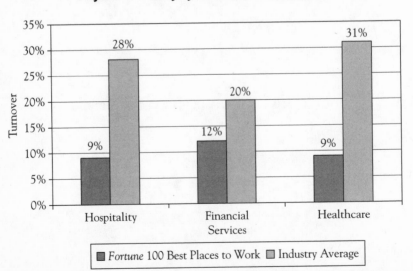

Figure 1.4 Engagement and Turnover

Source: Performancepoint, LLC, created using U.S. Department of Labor Statistics/ *Fortune* magazine 2006

Even more concerning is the practice of keeping employees who have already left, but remain in the building. There are a number of employees who skate by or have their minds occupied by other things. Only 62 percent of employees say they are regularly creative and resourceful, and only 38 percent say they are going to stick around in their current workplace. One of the most striking things we found in the Performancepoint survey is that 50 percent of the respondents said they are at 60 percent or less utilization of their capabilities in their performance on the job. Imagine the millions in payroll we are wasting.[21]

Productivity

Everyone is working harder these days, and no one doubts that work is more stressful. It most certainly is! So why ask how productive we are? Well, productivity is about a lot more than the number of hours people work or the number of tasks checked off a to-do list. Productivity relates to how connected each employee is to the mission of the organization. Are they working on the right stuff? Productivity is also about driving the business forward, taking educated risks, and being resourceful. Over and over again, we find organizations that have cultures hindering this type of productivity. It is a shame when employees and leaders are more concerned, literally and figuratively, with punching the time clock than with the quality of their work.

On one of our interventions it became clear that people were not working on the right things, even though they felt busy. (See Figure 1.5.) The employees at this company were stretched for time and wanted more support. Leadership was disappointed with the current performance of the sales group. There were a number of reasons why this client was not performing at a higher level. However, we found that the salespeople were not focused or proactive in their sales activities. We were able to identify, with the client, what would make the difference in sales and help the sales group shift their time to

Figure 1.5 Percentage Change in Key Activities at Client Organization

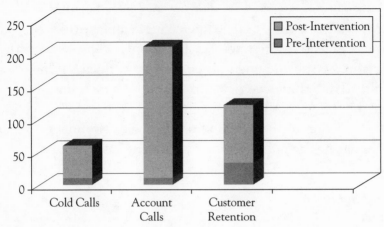

Source: Performancepoint, LLC

those activities. After working with the client, we were able to document significant changes in their productivity. Specifically, we saw significant increases in the number of cold calls and existing account calls, and an increase in customer retention rates.

Revenue and Profitability

The bottom line is that businesses need to make money. Executives are concerned with financials and we are driven by those financials, sometimes to our detriment. We can forget that we have been successful because we met a client or customer need. We were successful because our employees were motivated to meet the customer need. When we see the financials as the indicator of our success, we are too late. Financials are like the rearview mirror in our car. Once we look at our financial statements, we are looking at a picture of the past. These numbers represent earlier actions as an organization. The moment

Figure 1.6 The Bottom Line

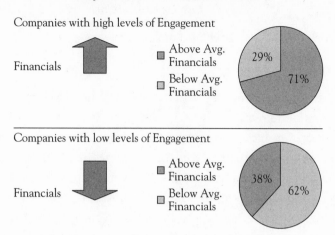

Source: Adapted from Corporate Leadership Council, a division of The Conference Executive Board Company, 2004 Employee Engagement Study

we react (or often overreact) to our financials, we make short-term decisions to achieve fiscal responsibility, forgetting that the very reason we have come to this place is because we took our eyes off of our real business and that reducing expenses will not create that connection again. Let me share with you an example of just how connected employee engagement is to success. More importantly, it is the significant lead indicator to success, as seen in Figure 1.6.

As you can see from the research completed by the Conference Board shown in Figure 1.6, companies with high levels of engagement outperform their competitors. These results have been proven over and over again based not only on revenue, but also on stock price[22] with an increase of 64 percent versus 21 percent, based on the company's ability to be employee friendly. One study demonstrated that people practices determined the likelihood of an IPO to survive past five years.[23]

In *engaged* organizations employees:

• Focus on getting the job done, but also on what is next;

• Feel a part of a team and something larger than themselves;

- Feel sharp and have less pressure to make employment jumps; and
- Work through change and approach fear in a mature manner.

Why do employees feel differently in some organizations versus others? The reason has to do with the organization's perspective of what employee engagement is and how it is prioritized.

When my company, Performancepoint, first started working on employee engagement issues, we were struck by how many different ways engagement was defined. Many organizations still look at employee engagement as satisfaction or a happiness rating, while others see it connected to issues such as union activity and absenteeism. Our concern with these approaches had to do with the fact that employee engagement was not seen as a business driver. These old definitions are tactical, stop-gap measures, and in the case of employee satisfaction can be seen as soft.

After much deliberation and research, we have defined employee engagement as:

> The **degree** to which a **person commits** to an organization and the **impact** that commitment has on how profoundly they **perform** and their length of **tenure**.

It is important to note that engagement is not an on/off switch. It is a continuum, and we will have employees who fall in various places on the continuum. The key to engagement is to move employees further along that continuum over time, as seen in Figure 1.7.

We are not talking about moving mountains. Small percentages of people moving toward stronger engagement levels can make significant differences in the workplace. Unfortunately, opportunities for movement are typically overlooked. One of the challenges we face as employers is that it is easier to focus on labels rather than on movement. When we view a picture of our

Figure 1.7 Client Year-Over-Year Employee Engagement Distribution Change

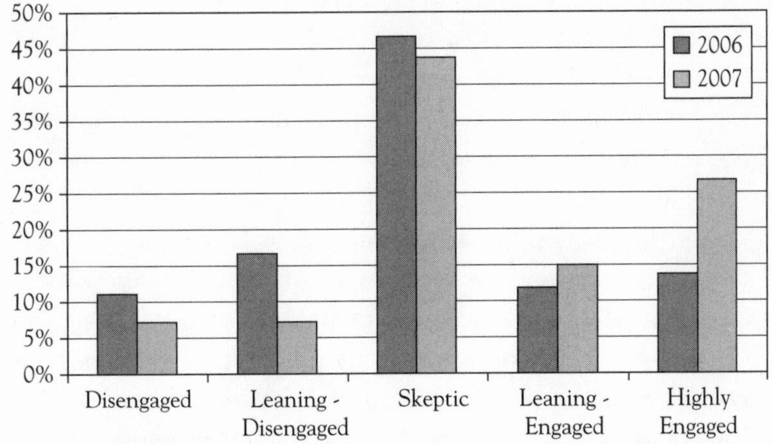

Source: Performancepoint, LLC

employee population and notice how few of our employees are engaged, we can become disappointed, even upset. Then when we zero in and see portions of our employees as disengaged, we may react even more. It is not uncommon to hear some clients say, "If those employees don't like working here, they can leave" or "These people will never change. They are just wired that way." There is nothing wrong with acknowledging when we have a less than stellar fit between an employee and the organization or arguing that a particular employee is just not wired for high engagement, yet that is not what we are discussing here.

Many organizations rest their success on the shoulders of a few, leaving room for a stronger commitment from a majority of the organization; in some cases 85 percent or more. Even the truly disengaged portions of an organizational population can reach upwards of 15 percent in many organizations. When we do not personalize the issue and we try not to connect individual faces to the feedback, we begin to see the data differently. We no longer see challenging people as the issue and we can start to see significant portions of the population as being left behind or not included. When we reexamine the issue from this perspective we can begin to ask, "What systemically is going on?" and "Are we okay with the current situation?" Now we are making a conscious choice. And when we make conscious choices like this, most of the time we choose movement rather than labels. The next question we should ask to create movement is: "How can we create more commitment?"

According to Wikipedia, commitment means duty or pledge to something or someone.[24] Other words or synonyms we could use to describe commitment might be "dedication," "devotion," or "responsibility." Commitment is all about engagement and accountability. The more committed we are, the more engaged and accountable we are. People make commitments to themselves, to others, and to ideas. Those commitments are sometimes implicit and other times explicit. We even make unconscious commitments. The most important idea behind commitment is that there can be many commitments made at any given time. We can commit to our work, career, team, the business strategy, the vision or mission, senior leadership, an idea, a project— and the list goes on.

Unfortunately, organizations have typically focused on one commitment—the commitment between the employee and the manager. However, the more commitments an employee has with an organization, the more likely the relationship will be stronger and last longer. Every commitment we make as employees, or in life for that matter, is based on a set of connections. A connection means "a joining or being joined; a relationship; association; the relation between things that depend on, involve, or follow each other."[25] Synonyms for connection are "link," "reciprocity," or "attachment." So a commitment is a dedication based on a connection(s), which represents a mutually beneficial bond. The big question for organizations then should be: "How do we create an environment that encourages connections or mutually beneficial bonds?"

If we look at the idea of connections from a different angle, it illustrates the point well. Each of us lives in a city, a place we call home, that may be temporary, or for some fairly permanent. It is precisely because of this willingness or unwillingness to move that one of the first questions recruiters ask usually has to do with a candidate's willingness to relocate for a particular position. Why is there a difference in preference between individuals? The answer is based on the number and strength of the connections the individual has with the city in which he or she lives. (See Figure 1.8.)

If I live in a city where my family lives, I have probably developed strong friendships. I may have a place of worship that

Figure 1.8 Connections

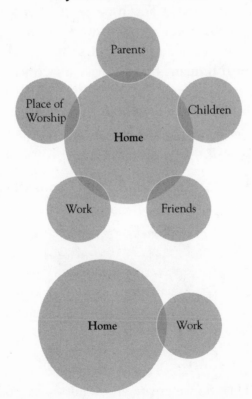

Source: Performancepoint, LLC

I attend where I am comfortable. And if I have a good job, then uprooting is difficult. If you add to that a sentimental liking of the area and a history, thirty years of experiences, I would have an even more thorny decision to make. If you then add in the additional detail that my children are in the crucial education years and moving them at this time would be more traumatic than when they were younger, then I have an intensely grueling decision on my hands and probably will not uproot. On the other hand, if all I have keeping me in a certain place is my job; then moving to another location is a less complicated decision because jobs are easily replaceable; unless this job is my dream job. It is for this very reason that the number of connections a person has to a city is only half the picture. The strength of a connection is just as relevant, because one connection can trump just about everything else. For instance, if I lived in a city and had a number of connections, most of which were strong, and I could not imagine leaving at all because this was where I wanted to live, I might still move. I might make a sacrifice for my strongest connection—a spouse who has an important career opportunity; a parent in need of physical assistance; a moral, ethical, or safety choice such as testifying in court and entering a witness

Figure 1.9 Commitment and Connections

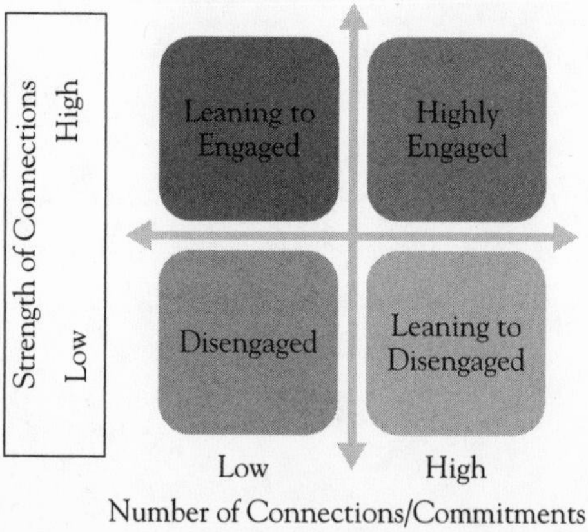

Strength of Connections: High / Low

Leaning to Engaged | Highly Engaged

Disengaged | Leaning to Disengaged

Low — High

Number of Connections/Commitments

protection program; or maybe for children, to take advantage of an opportunity to improve their future. (See Figure 1.9.)

Impact is also very important. Most organizations attempt to measure employee engagement and rarely, if ever, tie it to their businesses. Some stop at some kind of a satisfaction measure. Unfortunately, satisfaction is a fickle measure that changes quickly and frequently. The reason satisfaction measures are fickle is due to the emotional nature of these types of measures. Feelings are quick to change and vary in intensity. Most importantly, feelings are based on connections and beliefs. If we measure bonds and the beliefs these bonds are made up of, then we are more likely to obtain a stable and more accurate reading of the environment. An example of the difference might be

Feeling Measure: "I like working at ABC Organization."

Connection Measure: "I believe my organization has a culture of integrity."

The first measure is interesting, yet tells us very little because it can change daily or hourly based on the most recent events. The second measure, the connection measure, begins to tell a story. What you can do as an organization is to ask both types of questions and use the correlation between the two to try to demonstrate cause and effect. However, an even more powerful approach, especially at the executive level, is to tie the measures to real impact.

We want to measure strong indicators of success: productivity, retention, customer loyalty, profitability, and revenue. When I use the word "productivity," I am not referring to the number of hours an employee works or how busy he or she is. I am referring to the person's creativity, resourcefulness, and ability to work on what counts. I do not mean to imply that employee satisfaction is not important. We want a happy and healthy workplace. I am just saying that if we create a company in which people stick around and are comfortable being creative and resourceful, then we have created a healthy and accountability-driven environment. Accountability or ownership is essential; otherwise, our employees become victims and we develop an ineffective culture over time. Those organizations that worry about satisfaction become more interested in making employees happy, sometimes bypassing the necessary discomfort that comes with change and reducing accountability in the process. More importantly, when our measurement factors consistently lead to success, we have now created a hard financial reason for an organization to treat its employees with as much importance as it does marketing, advertising, financials, and other functions that reside at the executive table.

Questions to Ask Yourself

- What connections do we have with our employees?
- What reasons, emotions, and aspirations do we provide our employees with which they can connect?
- How could we create different types of connections with our employees?
- What have we done that would reduce the bond we have with our employees?
- How have we focused on movement toward stronger engagement levels?
- How have we focused on labels and lost sight of the bigger picture?
- What impact have our engagement efforts had on productivity?
- How have our engagement efforts improved customer loyalty?
- How have we improved the organization's results through our engagement efforts?

2

IT'S NOT JUST THE MANAGER, STUPID!

Most organizations spend time and money collecting employee engagement data each year. In some cases, organizations collect data on a quarterly, or even a monthly, basis. So the natural question is, "What are we getting for that investment?" The unfortunate answer for many organizations is "very little." I would argue that many of the surveys and tools utilized to measure employee engagement are flawed in their design and doomed to failure before they start. Even among the tools that do work, many are only helpful for a couple of years before a company plateaus or even falls backward without any wisdom for turning the results around.

Factors Impacting Engagement Data

For years we have heard, "It's the manager, stupid." I have often wondered why the manager/employee relationship has been highlighted as the reason for employee engagement issues. Well, I am here to say, "It's not just the manager, stupid! It's the manager and a host of other things." Much of the survey design and development strategy being utilized today starts with a premise that limits success—the hard focus on the manager being just one example. Hear me out, and I will share what I mean.

Narrow Research

Typically, two types of employee engagement research are referenced (see Figure 2.1). The first type is multi-company research that compares the engagement levels among different organizations, usually in the same industry. However, a great deal of employee engagement research has focused on studying one company in-depth. This type of research is more common because it is challenging to get permission from many companies to collect data about the organizations and their employees. So we tend to settle on collecting data from one organization. We call this "single company research," and much of this research

Figure 2.1 Two Ways to Measure Engagement

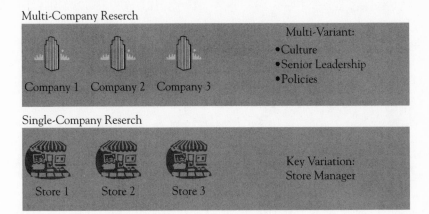

Source: Performancepoint, LLC

has focused on the retail industry because it is easier to show bottom-line results when we compare financial performance across stores. So far, single company approaches sound good, but let's take a further look at how this approach plays out. If we were to study one chain, let's say Starbucks for example, and compared each Starbucks unit or store with another, what would really be different? Very little would differ between stores; compensation model, not really; benefits, no, store design, negligible. The main difference between stores would be the manager of the individual Starbucks location.

Now, if you looked at Starbucks and compared it with another organization, say Dunkin' Donuts, we would see a very different story. A number of areas would differ, such as:

- Culture
- Senior leadership
- Goal setting
- Strategy
- Work environment
- Compensation

- Benefits
- Store design
- Innovation
- Knowledge management
- Selection and on-boarding
- Communication mechanisms
- Recognition

Clearly, the manager or direct supervisor is an important factor in the employee engagement equation. The direct supervisor, however, is not the entire footprint of employee engagement. Another way to explore this concept is through viewing a picture (see Figure 2.1). We could look at a picture—the headshot of an individual. What do we know about this person from this picture? Not very much, but we can observe a few things. This individual is most likely in his forties, has a goatee, dark hair, and is male. What if we could learn more?

The picture is actually a cropped view of a larger picture. When we view the original picture we can see several individuals. Two individuals in the picture appear to be married. We know this not only because we can now see the woman in the picture, but also because the two adults are both wearing wedding rings and are accompanied by two children. The oldest child looks about eight, so most likely they have been married for at least nine years. What is the difference between what this view and the earlier, cropped picture reveal?

The more complete picture is the second one. We see and learn more about the individual from the broader view. While both pictures appear complete, the second provides more insight. Research is no different. When we utilize single company research, we may feel good about the observations we receive. We may even feel as though we are gaining answers. However, when we use this approach as a starting point, we are losing the bigger picture, important insights, and the wisdom to create sustainable results.

One could make the argument that being focused allows an organization to zero in on one area and have a stronger, more pinpointed impact; however, to assess the impact of this approach you would have to ask yourself, "Is that the best area to magnify?" The only way to answer that question is to look at the broad view first and then focus on the priorities.

Poor Survey Design

A second area that tends to lead us astray is poor survey design. We had a prospect call us a couple of years ago wanting to explore using our tool. When we inquired about the tool they

Figure 2.2 Missing the Big Picture

Source: Performancepoint, LLC

were using, we were told that it wasn't adding a lot of value. After taking a look at the survey, it was clear why. Many of the items were written in a manner that created problems, rather than promoting solutions.

In this case, and in most others, the questions dealt with items such as compensation. The compensation questions all referred in some way to satisfaction with pay, and every year that was the key issue that came up in the survey results. The quirk of fate was that the company could not change its business model, many of the employees were paid hourly and were far from well-off financially, and the organization actually brought more attention to the pay issue by doing the survey. After two or three years, this was starting to have a negative impact on the organization's engagement levels because it kept raising an issue the organization could not solve.

Some other questions or items aside from compensation are not helpful to ask. (See Exhibit 2.1.) Most of the time these

Exhibit 2.1 Examples of Poorly Designed Survey Questions and Rating Scales

Item	Concern
The pay I receive for my type of work is as good as other companies pay.	The answer to a question like this is usually no.
I feel my benefits are as good as other companies give.	The answer to a question like this is usually no.
I am paid enough for the work that I do.	The answer to a question like this is usually no.
I have sufficient time to complete my activities.	The answer to a question like this is usually no.
I am allowed time to maintain competency in my primary area of specialization.	Not appropriate for significant percentage of the employee population. Either generalists or specialists will rate this item poorly.

| I look forward to going to work on Mondays. | The answer to a question like this is usually no. |
| I have a friend at work. | Difficult and sometimes impractical to act on. |

Poor Rating Scale: Too Much Gradation
Extremely satisfied
Satisfied
Somewhat satisfied
Neither satisfied or dissatisfied
Somewhat dissatisfied
Dissatisfied
Extremely satisfied
Not applicable

Poor Rating Scale: Too Little Gradation
Satisfied
Unsatisfied
Neither

Productive Rating Scale
Strongly agree
Agree
Slightly agree
Slightly disagree
Disagree
Strongly disagree
Not applicable (included on appropriate items)

Source: Performancepoint, LLC

types of questions fail to measure much of anything, are biased in and of themselves, or lead to feedback that is impractical on which to act. Another problem with poorly designed surveys is the rating scale. Certain rating scales are not clear, have too much gradation, focus on satisfaction rather than agreement or degree of accuracy, or offer too many "outs" for an employee when providing a rating. Some words of advice when reviewing items for inclusion:

- Remove items that will most likely illicit specific answers regardless if the situation. These types of items will bias the survey results.

- Questions or items should generally not need explanations. Understandably, there are people who desire more explanation than others, but the items should be fairly easy to understand.

- Items on a survey should relate to all or a majority of respondents. If an item does not relate to most employees, it should be placed in a separate section of the survey. These types of items should be limited. Most importantly, make sure these items still relate to a large number of employees and will not be utilized or perceived to be utilized to identify people.

- Each question should measure one main idea. When measuring more than one idea with a question, we can be clear on the results, but not what the results mean. Before we ask a question we should be clear on what we are measuring.

- Limit the use of the choices "neutral" or "not applicable." These choices allow employees an opportunity to avoid providing an opinion. Certain questions may need a "not applicable" option, such as "I had an opportunity to discuss the previous organizational survey results with a member of management," or "ABC Company is a better place to work this year than it was last year." Obviously, if a new employee is filling out the survey, he or she will not have an opinion on these items. However, on an item such as, "My manager is receptive to new ideas," most employees will have a perspective or belief.

Biased Approach

My organization encourages clients to use a third party, even if it is not us, for organizational surveys. I will get to the reasons later. Having said this, I will also caution you to clearly look at the approach you are taking with the third party. It never ceases to amaze me how many consulting firms have one or two solutions and, miraculously, their assessment identifies a need for exactly the solutions they offer. Even the research they use to justify the validity of their tool is based on their approach, rather than on the state of the employee engagement arena as a whole. When using a vendor to do an organizational survey, check for the following:

- References of research from other sources;
- Multiple product offerings in a variety of employee engagement touch points, or a sole focus on surveying;
- Questions in the survey about issues for which the vendor does not provide solutions;
- A comprehensive perspective on employee engagement;
- A clear employee engagement business model;
- Strong analysis rather than just numbers; and
- Use of research that is tied to hard measures such a revenue, customer loyalty, and/or profits.

Poor survey design, including bias toward a particular aspect of employee engagement such as the direct supervisor, can mask larger issues and cause employee engagement to decrease over time.

Engagement Drivers

So what should be a part of any organizational assessment? What is important to the success of an entity? After reviewing numerous studies and doing some of our own research, we have come up with the following systems, processes, and factors that serve as drivers of employee engagement (see Figure 2.3).

Culture

What are our shared norms? Culture is derived from the Latin word *colere*, which means "to cultivate"[1,2] At work in our

Figure 2.3 Drivers of Employee Engagement

Culture	Success Indicators
Priority Setting	Communication
Innovation	Talent Acquisition
Talent Enhancement	Customer/Business Cycles

Incentives and Acknowledgement

Employee Engagement

Source: Performancepoint, LLC

organizations, we cultivate certain types of behavior patterns or shared norms. Sometimes these behavior patterns are more or less similar to the ones we espouse. Many organizations use the term "values" to describe their espoused or desired culture. The larger the variance between the espoused and the actual culture, the more likely employee engagement is negatively impacted. Organizations engage in culture change projects all the time. Too many times, the culture change efforts are reflected in fanfare, posters, and big announcements without any significant changes in the way an organization operates. Whether the disconnect is caused by a lack of execution, an unwillingness to make difficult decisions, or hope that the employees will just "get us there" does not really matter. What does matter is that employees feel deflated by the disconnect and distrust the environment when "what is said" and "what is done" do not match.

Success Indicators

Every organization should have a clear way to measure success that translates to all its key stakeholders, and especially to its employees.

Questions to Ask Yourself

- What kind of culture do we espouse?
- What kind of culture actually exists?
- What is the difference between the espoused culture and the actual culture?
- How does our culture impact client/customer relationships?
- How does our culture impact our success?
- How does our culture impact trust in our organization?

Metrics are a tool for measuring success. Most organizations utilize financials to determine performance. However, financials are a backward (past view) and outcome-based look at performance. Financials will not provide insight into how well you are delivering on your promise currently. Without clear success indicators that tie to each person's work, employees will fail to bring everything they can to the job every day.

Questions to Ask Yourself

- What are our success measurements?
- How well are these success measures known and shared throughout the organization?
- To what extent do the success measures align with each other?
- To what extent do these success measures align with our culture?
- How well balanced are our success measures?
- To what extent do our success measures relate to the value we bring to our customers?

Priority Setting

Goal setting is a natural part of every operation. Some organizations do it well, and others struggle. How engaged your people are depends greatly on how priority setting works in your organization. Organizations that are able to define clear priorities and goals and gain buy-in from various aspects of the organization leverage the resources they can bear and the energy their employees can put forth. Organizations operate on limited budgets and resources. Each of us, as an employee, has a wish list that typically needs to be pared down to reality. When those limited resources are diffused, our branding can get lost, product introductions can be delayed, quality standards can be lowered, and our people can burn out or become disenchanted.

Communication

Communication systems are an integral part of a daily operation. Organizations have formal communication systems and

Questions to Ask Yourself

- Are priorities and goals set at the top and part of an exclusive club?
- Are priorities and goals shared or marketed to employees?
- Are they developed by the entire organization in a participative manner?
- How often do priorities change?
- Are there too many priorities to work toward?
- When priorities need to change, how does this occur? Who is involved?
- When priorities are in conflict, how is resolution achieved?
- Can individuals see the direct link between their individual and department goals, and the goals of the organization?

structures, as well as informal communication systems and structures. Some organizations leverage these systems, and others are held hostage by them. The more clear, concise, and compelling our communication systems are, the more likely we are to be able to drive our goals forward.

Another aspect of communication revolves around social networking, collaboration, and coordination. Many organizations are turning to the use of technology, specifically tools such as wikis, to involve their employees, reduce the need for travel, and accommodate the different schedules, shifts, and time zones represented by their employees.

Employees value candor and honesty in the messaging they receive. However, sometimes messages do not get through. How we gain our employees' attention is as important as what we communicate and the clarity with which it is communicated. All three aspects of communication are of particular importance.

A good indicator that corporations struggle with balancing these three aspects of communicating is the current use of wikis. Almost all of the Fortune 500 companies are using wikis, but not many of them have a strategy for their use.[3]

Questions to Ask Yourself

- What information is communicated openly?
- What information is held closely or hoarded?
- What information is more credible—information coming from informal or formal sources?
- To what extent do we send mixed messages to our employees?
- How have we utilized repetition to ensure messages are received?
- How many different types of communication vehicles does our organization utilize?

- To what extent are we aware of and understand our informal communication networks?
- To what extent do we communicate the right messages, in the right way, at the right time?

Innovation

Innovation too many times is viewed from the lens of "invent." When we think of innovation in this manner, we leave progress to people wearing white coats in laboratories. Instead, we should embrace innovation as a way of working in which every day each of us should be advancing, progressing, and building upon our past successes.[4] These incremental changes or movements mean much more to most businesses than trying to leapfrog the competition. The core skills related to innovation are problem solving, creativity, and collaboration. However, organizations with these skill sets still have difficulty with innovating, typically because the environment does not foster innovation, change, or creativity. In certain organizations, it is easier and safer to keep your head down and do what you are told. Having strong accountability and being allowed a certain amount of freedom and safety to learn from your mistakes are essential ingredients to stirring innovation.

Talent Acquisition

We live and die each day based on how we work with our clients and what we deliver to them. In the end, our products and services are created and delivered by our associates—our talent. It is astonishing how many organizations talk a good game when it comes to selection and on-boarding, but do not deliver the goods on a consistent basis. Selection and on-boarding are

---

Questions to Ask Yourself

- How are our problem solving and collaborative skill sets?
- How have we helped each employee see their role in innovating?
- What gets in our way with regard to innovating?
- What systems have we put in place to help us solve problems and collaborate?
- To what extent do we value and even foster creativity?
- To what extent have we created an environment that rewards "out of the box" thinking?
- To what extent does bureaucracy limit our ability to maintain a competitive edge?
- How safe is it to take educated risks in this environment?
- To what extent do we value new, unproven ideas?

---

fantastic tools to brand your company, reduce learning curves, promote early successes, increase productivity, and reduce attrition. And if well-thought-out, selection and on-boarding practices serve as public relations tools as well.

Talent Enhancement

Growing our people and increasing organizational knowledge are vital ingredients to staying competitive. We often provide training to our employees, especially for core skills, but do we truly prepare our people with the skills they need to grow, develop, and change over time? We can work very hard learning a job for five years and become obsolete, or we can work very hard at growing our skill sets and we can be more valuable.

Another area of talent enhancement revolves around knowledge management. Knowledge management reflects the

---

Questions to Ask Yourself

- How are we currently branding ourselves using our recruiting and selection systems? How should we?
- To what extent does our selection process identify the right people?
- How well are we doing at on-boarding new talent?
- How do we create early successes for each new employee?
- What happens after orientation?
- To what extent does our process place responsibility on the candidate for making a productive decision?
- What do people think of us after interviewing for a job and getting it? And not getting it?
- How does it feel to be a candidate for a job at our organization?
- How does it feel to be a new employee at our organization?

---

organization's ability to collect, document, and make available intellectual knowledge. The idea of a strong knowledge management approach is to build on capability over time, regardless of who stays and who goes. Without a strong knowledge management system, many organizations find themselves introducing policies that have previously failed, altering processes that have already shown value, and reengaging vendors that have already been tried and found inappropriate.[5] Knowledge management is another area where wikis can be extremely helpful.

Incentives and Acknowledgement

We spend a great deal of time putting together elaborate compensation structures based on the market and comparisons to other organizations, minimizing risk based on legal ramifications, maximizing profit, or minimizing costs. In many cases,

Questions to Ask Yourself

- When people leave, how much history and knowledge walk out the door with them?

- Where are we over-reliant on an expert or specialist to get information?

- Where are our bottlenecks due to reliance on people in key positions?

- What have we accomplished with our knowledge management? Shorter product development cycles? Shorter sales cycles? Process sustainability?

- How do we currently store, access, and learn from our history as an entity?

these compensation structures become complicated, politicized, and ineffective. Countless times, we have seen compensation structures that incent the wrong behavior, or at least a different behavior than intended.

Acknowledgement is different from recognition. It is, in its purest sense, more authentic. We should not recognize employees because we have to, or because it is a good tool. These employees come to work every day, many times sacrificing life/work balance and filled with anxiety because of pressure, and we forget that. We should acknowledge their efforts not as a strategy, but because it is right to do so. And we can only do this well if we truly are grateful for their efforts. In this day and age, we have come to expect our employees to be grateful that they have a job, which only serves to make them feel less appreciated.

Customer-Centered

Businesses start out by focusing on a customer need and providing some value along the way. Over time, a business can become a slave to growth/numbers, minimizing risk, or making life easier from its own perspective, and forget the reason why the business

Questions to Ask Yourself

- How well does our compensation system really work? What are the challenges or problems that our system creates?

- How many experienced people do we lose because we pay new hires more than existing employees?

- Are our compensation systems too complicated?

- Are we truly incenting behavior that drives the business forward? How equitable and inclusive is our compensation system?

- To what extent has our compensation system been compromised by politics?

- To what degree are we grateful that we have the employees we do?

- To what degree does our leadership authentically acknowledge our employees' efforts?

was successful in the first place. The customer interface should always be sacred and driven by the customers' preferences and buying cycles.

There have always been arguments made regarding changing customer behavior. While we can influence our customers, we must keep in mind that long-term sustainability is dependent on a relationship that has value for both parties. We can ask customers to do things for us, as long as there is something in it for them. There is a reason we have the J.D. Power awards and other service markers for which we, as businesses, compete. Businesses that are built to revolve around customers and create a positive and intuitive customer experience will outperform those that are not.

Employees also have a voice on this subject, as well. Most employees want to do a good job and prefer to make customers happy. When employees see their own organization as lacking customer focus, they doubt the integrity of the organization as a whole. In some cases, employees will begin to feel a sense of shame and will long for the pride they want to feel as they work. Remember, customer preferences come first!

Global to Local Lenses

Each of these business structures/systems can be viewed from a number of lenses. Employee engagement is impacted by a number of factors. Employees connect to broad ideas and to people. We suggest the following four levels from which to view employee engagement and the data collected by an organization:

Questions to Ask Yourself

- To what extent are we trying to change consumer behavior versus meet a customer need?
- To what extent does stock price, shareholder value, and so forth drive organizational behavior over actual business cycles or customer interests?
- How customer-centric is our business?
- To what degree is our organizational structure supporting customer interests and business cycles?
- What value are we bringing to our customers?
- What made our business successful in the first place? To what extent have we stayed connected to our origins?
- To what extent has bureaucracy impacted our customer relationships?
- To what extent have we acted consistently, both internally and externally, regarding our customers?

- *Leadership/Organization:* What systemic issues can we resolve or leverage to drive engagement? How can we utilize employee engagement to create an organizational dialogue and promote transparency?

- *Direct Supervisor/Manager:* What can our leaders do to help employees create connections and provide a healthy daily experience? How can our managers balance their own individual needs with the their responsibilities for employee engagement

- *Team:* What can our teams do to support strong problem solving, collaboration, and inclusion? How can teams create the type of work environment that fosters employee engagement?

- *Individual:* How can each individual create and sustain connections at work? How can they help others to do so as well? How can employees learn to increase ownership/accountability and their ability to change?

We tend to provide reports that illustrate organizational needs and then break them down by department/function, or demographics. All of this information is important. However, if your approach allows you to see how a function, group, team, or demographic sees itself, the direct manager, and the organization, then the instrument is even more powerful because it is no longer just rolling up or breaking down the data. Now you are able to actually see variances in the data that help you to know where to focus. (See Exhibit 2.2.)

Why These Drivers Are Important

The drivers serve as a performance indicator rather than a win/loss metric. They help us stay focused on the business through our people. Imagine looking at your car dashboard. We utilize the dashboard to determine whether we are safe driving the car, compliant with

Exhibit 2.2 Global to Local

There are some distinct differences between the different sub-groups. Each area should spend some time reflecting on its specific opportunities. We would encourage dialogue with employees and involving them in working through these opportunities.

Specifically, here is a breakdown by age:

- **18 to 29:** This group is concerned with compensation and getting the necessary information needed to do the job. Generally speaking, these individuals want to be able to accomplish their tasks and be paid accordingly. Some of the individuals in this group feel challenged with the lack of information sharing and the fairness of the compensation structure.

- **30 to 40:** This group is more concerned with issues regarding a safe culture and trust in senior leadership. They also believe that the on-boarding process for new employees needs improvement.

- **40 to 49:** Having a coach or mentor is very important to this group. They would like to have such a relationship to grow themselves and increase their contribution to ABC Company. Another area of concern for this segment is trust in senior leadership.

- **50 to 59:** This group is the first group to bring up their direct supervisor as a potential concern. Specifically, some see direct supervisors putting themselves before their employees. This is a key concern because it is a very high-impact item when it comes to turnover and productivity. They also believe that ABC Company needs to be more inclusive and innovative.

- **60 to 69:** The major areas of concern for this group is senior leadership. They believe senior leadership can be more open to new ideas and focus more on the employees' needs. They see less improvement in ABC Company being a better place to work and in living the "ABC" values.

Source: Performancepoint, LLC

the speed limits and law, and whether we have enough gas. Each of those indicators will change; going up or down at various times, and that is okay. However, when one of those areas becomes unacceptable, dangerous, a distraction, or limiting, we must make a change, such as adding gasoline or getting the car serviced. Sometimes circumstances also change the way we view the car dashboard. If we are driving locally versus making a four-hundred-and-twenty-mile trip, we may choose to act differently. For instance, before the trip we inspect the car's fluids, put air in the tires, change the oil, and fill the car with gas. The same is true for our organizations and people. The way we view the data and how we act may be impacted by circumstances on the ground such as a merger, a drop in stock price, a difficult economy, or a change in leadership. We must have a dashboard that allows us to do the following.

Focus our capacity. We, individually and collectively, have only so much energy. We can dilute our efforts or make them stronger by creating focus. Capacity is like the idea of volume. A coffee mug will only hold so much liquid. Each day when you fill that coffee mug it will only hold the same amount of liquid. When we pour in too much liquid it overflows, we create a mess, and lose much of the coffee we brewed. If we under-fill the mug, we will fill up our time making unnecessary trips to refill the mug. Work is no different. We pour too much work on many, and all we do is lose momentum because their cups runneth over. When we pour too little work on a person, he or she will find a way to fill the day. Another challenge is the lack of clarity regarding work. Most of us have too much work, so we choose which work on which to concentrate. In some cases, we choose a different set of priorities than what the organization needs due to personal preference, comfort levels, and lack of clarity regarding what counts. We see this time and again with salespeople who need to prospect as a part of their job, but choose not to, because they dislike the rejection. If a sales division does not make prospecting a priority, salespeople will concentrate on other types of activities—some of which won't drive the success of the organization.

Optimize our resources. Organizations are made up of structures and systems. We have spent our time trying get as much out of every department, function, and system as possible. What if we should be approaching work differently? What if we purposely make a choice that would actually help the overall function of the organization, but to do that we have to outsource a function, sub-optimize an area of the company, or focus on a segment of our employee population rather than the whole? Which levers at our disposal will help us better deliver those results? How can we get certain departments to truly serve other departments rather than compete? In order to accomplish this goal, the customer must be front and center, egos will need to be checked at the door, politics will have to be limited, and transparency and dialogue must be a part of the daily operation.

Deliberately evolve. The world changes around us and organizations typically survive, even if we hit tumultuous times. Yes, things have become more difficult and competitive, but with major efforts and changes we make it through. Unfortunately, this is disruptive, and we leave many colleagues behind in the process. What if we purposely or proactively changed, even when there was no existing significant or urgent pain? This would require equipping our employees with new skill sets, a more ongoing investment of time and money, reducing our time in the comfort zone, and a deliberate focus on what is coming next. But when change feels more like a major accident rather than an ongoing effort, it becomes unhelpful and costly.

When we view our engagement drivers from this perspective, we become less interested in being perfect, attaining a great score, year-over-year comparisons, and even in our competitive comparisons. What does become crystal clear is the importance of the journey and having a set of measures that help us understand where we are and what we need to do in the next business cycle or annual period to support our people and profits. (See Figure 2.4.)

Knowing what to measure and the benefits to measuring key drivers is a good first step. It is imperative that we look at employee engagement through a broader lens and search past

Figure 2.4 Engagement Benefits

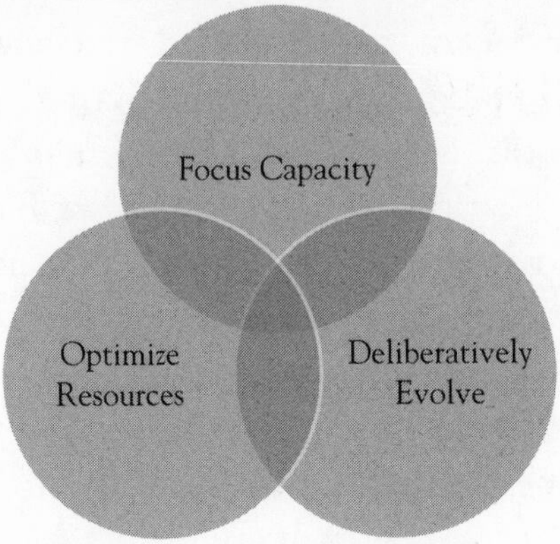

Focus Capacity

Optimize Resources

Deliberatively Evolve

Source: Performancepoint, LLC

the basic drivers such as the manager, that we ask productive questions, and that we ask people to provide feedback using appropriate rating scales. Once we have a survey or tool with which we feel comfortable, gaining wisdom from the data becomes the next challenge.

Where are you on your employee engagement journey as an organization? Take the quick down-and-dirty assessment in Exhibit 2.3 by checking the most appropriate box by the driver.

Exhibit 2.3 Employee Engagement Assessment

Engagement Driver	Perfect	Acceptable	Concern	Dangerous
Culture				
Success Indicators				
Priority Setting				
Communication				
Innovation				
Talent Acquisition				
Talent Enhancement				
Incentives and Acknowledgement				
Customer-Centered				
Global to Local Lenses				

3

MEASURE TWICE, CUT ONCE

Whenever I have started a home improvement project by checking my plans and measurements before I purchased materials or commenced the work, at each step this was the difference between success and failure, being at budget or over budget, or between one trip to Lowe's versus five trips to Lowe's. My father-in-law, Bill, helped me with many of the home improvement projects I undertook. He always planned everything out to the tiniest detail and checked his plan multiple times. He made certain to analyze what he needed to do first, second, and then third; and then he would revisit the plan and revise his efforts along the way. Sometimes, I was impatient with the process, but it was a good process. Bill always would say, "Measure twice, cut once." What he was really saying was, "Knowing what you want to do and doing it are two very different things." I can have all of the information in front of me and execute my actions poorly. However, if I take the time to analyze all of the information in an effective manner, then I will most likely be successful.

Managing Engagement Surveys

Managing an employee engagement survey is very much the same. However, it is astonishing to me how often organizations plow through action steps after the data comes back without even looking back. When organizations utilize an organizational or engagement survey, most of the effort is spent on collecting data, and the process of taking actions to deliver results from the data can take on a life of its own.

Once the data has been collected, organizations race to do something with it. The old adage, "If you can't measure it, you can't manage it" is true. However, we must make sure we are managing the right things. Most efforts to measure employee engagement are focused on surveys that show ratings results provided by the employees. Organizations take a cue from those results and set action plans. Typically, organizations look at the items on the survey that were rated the highest and the lowest, and then focus on improving the scores that were low and emphasizing the ones that were rated more highly. There are times when organizations become paralyzed by all of the data they are provided and cannot make sense of it because they are overwhelmed by too much information. Sometimes, a consultant will provide intuitive advice in these situations, based on experience. We feel compelled in these cases to trust that the consultant is right, based more on intuition than on anything else. Please do not misunderstand what I am saying: intuition has its place, but if you have just invested significant time and energy on a survey project collecting data, then you should be able to truly interpret the data and gain some inherent wisdom from it.

What do we really know when we get back the results from an employee engagement survey? How do we know we are working

Figure 3.1 Filters for Employee Engagement

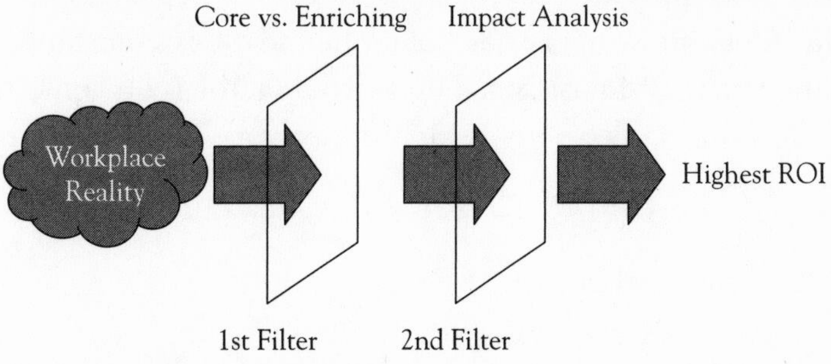

Core vs. Enriching   Impact Analysis

Workplace Reality

Highest ROI

1st Filter   2nd Filter

Source: Performancepoint, LLC

on the right initiatives? Which efforts will lead to real impact? Unfortunately, most organizations cannot answer these questions. That is why we recommend that organizations conduct a thorough analysis, instead of using the typical approaches, using two key filters for the data—Type and Impact. See Figure 3.1.

Types of Engagement Factors

Core Engagement Factors

There are two types of engagement factors that we have found to exist in the workplace. Our model is very similar to Herzberg's two-factor model as explained in Bolman and Deal (2008).[1] The first type of engagement factor is a "core" factor. We define "core" as a primary or essential factor in engagement. These are the basic necessities that must exist for employees to be productive in the work environment such as:

- Information and training
- Tools
- Supplies
- Appropriate policies and procedures
- Capable manager
- Reasonable benefits
- Compensation

Core factors reflect the idea that my manager, team, and organization provide me what I need to be successful. No employee wants to feel that his or her work circumstances are working against him or her. The second factor is an "enriching" factor. Enriching factors are highly motivational and are much more values driven, such as:

- Believing in what I do
- Believing in whom I work for
- Feeling that I make a difference
- Having a sense of trust
- Participating in a customer centric culture
- Enjoying an innovative environment
- Experiencing long-term career opportunities

See Figure 3.2 for some types of engagement.

Enriching Engagement Factors

Why look at the issues that drive engagement with this filter? Because we cannot work toward an enriching engagement

Figure 3.2 Types of Engagement

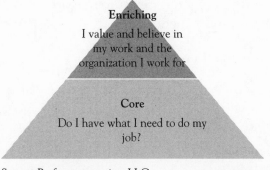

Source: Performancepoint, LLC

environment when our core engagement needs have not been met. To make a point, I will share a true and somewhat extreme story from an early part of my career. I had just taken a job with a large health insurance company. Prior to my actual start date, the organization instituted a budget freeze. So on my first day, I was shown my office. It was a very nice space, fairly spacious, and in a good location. The office was truly an office, not the cubicles you see so often today. It was clean and freshly painted. There were cabinets hung on the walls to store my belongings and supplies and plenty of file cabinets to keep myself organized. I couldn't have been happier; except for one thing . . . there was no desk. When I inquired about the desk, I was told there was a budget freeze and that my employer was unable to purchase a desk for me. When I questioned further, it was suggested to me that maybe I could temporarily work sitting on the floor, or see whether any-one would let the new guy share an office for an undefined period of time (I guess you know how that went over). Now, mind you, I felt a bit betrayed. How could they have hired me, asked me to start work, and not provided a basic necessity I needed to be effective? Not having a functional office space was a "core" need. I was not thinking about enriching engagement needs, such as my confidence and trust in senior leadership. I was thinking "How can I get a desk? Did I make a mistake taking this job? How can I be productive?"

Impact

The second filter is impact. (See Figure 3.3.) Based on whether an organization needs to focus on core or enriching engagement factors, it should then choose to work on the factors with the most leverage.

What will have the most impact over the next year? There are is only one way to achieve this goal. Connect your engage-ment factors to performance indicators such as revenue, prof-itability, productivity, and turnover. Some organizations turn

Figure 3.3 Example of Engagement Item Analysis

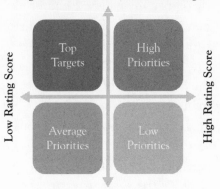

High Return on Investment Ranking

Low Rating Score

High Rating Score

Top Targets

High Priorities

Average Priorities

Low Priorities

Low Return on Investment Ranking

Source: Performancepoint, LLC

to consulting firms like ours that have already facilitated this process in a generic manner across many data points, and others want to create a more targeted correlation based on their business. Obviously, the second and more pinpointed way to determine impact, a validation study, is more expensive. Either way, this is a very different avenue from choosing items based on whether they were rated low versus rated high. We break down engagement indicators into four key categories.

Top Targets (Low Rating, High Impact). The items in this category represent what an organization will want to focus on during the next period; usually a year. These are items that receive low ratings from employees in a survey and also have the greatest impact on issues such as productivity, retention, and organizational results. Working on these particular issues will not only have the greatest impact on an organization's employee engagement results, but it will also have the maximum impact on the organization's success.

High Priorities (High Rating, High Impact). These items are important to leverage or maintain and should be an organization's next focus. These items received high ratings and also have significant impact on the organization's success. Consider these items strengths that are working to the organization's advantage. If these items fall backward in ratings, performance of the organization will suffer.

Average Priorities (Low Rating, Low Impact). These items reflect low ratings and low impact. Essentially, they are organizational weaknesses that have little impact on the performance of an organization. These items typically will not influence productivity or retention a great deal. However, any item(s) rated low should be reviewed to determine if there is a pattern in the ratings that tells a story, or there is a need to shore up a real weakness because it is getting in the way.

Low Priorities (High Rating, Low Impact). The items reflect strengths of an organization, because they are rated highly by employees on a survey, but they typically have little impact on issues like productivity, retention, and organizational results. While we try not to fall backward on these types of items, the impact of falling backward would most likely be negligible. We would not recommend an organization spend its time focusing in this area.

When we work with clients, there are times we need to steer them away from some of the items rated low because we know from our research that working on those items will not produce the results that addressing another item will. In order to achieve this type of analysis, each item must be tagged with the necessary information, such as the type of engagement indicator and the impact of the item.

In Table 3.1, we have shared an example that includes an impact ranking; with the scale that the lower the impact ranking number the higher the impact. Therefore, you can see from the chart that if we were to focus on Core Engagement, where the two items in the figure were rated low, we would want to focus

Table 3.1 Item Categorization

Item	Engagement Type	Impact/Ranking
My manager has the skills to do his/her job	Core	10
My manager rates my current performance accurately	Core	32
I want to work for my manager because (s)he has integrity and is honest	Enriching	6
I believe my manager is my advocate	Enriching	24

Source: Performancepoint, LLC

on the item with the impact rating of 10. However, if we were focusing on Enriching Engagement and both items were rated low, we would want put our energies toward the item with the impact ranking of 6.

When conducting a validation study, we recommend when possible connecting the engagement items to customer loyalty/ satisfaction figures, as well as organizational results. If we are to invest our monies, our limited budgets, shouldn't we choose the most important, leveragable actions? What we find is that many organizations spend a great deal of time collecting data, and then flip a coin, per se, in deciding how to deal with the information they receive.

Types of Surveys

Organizational Engagement Survey

Typically, you will find two types of surveys that can be utilized to measure employee engagement. The first type is an organizational assessment. In general, this is an annual assessment of an organization's employee engagement and how their standing impacts productivity, retention, and organizational health. An organizational assessment is much like going to the doctor and getting a full work-up or physical. We are trying to examine the state of affairs. The survey is characteristically open to the entire employee population and the desire is to get as much participation as possible. We have had clients reach as much as 96 percent of their employee population. We want to encourage as much participation as possible because, for many employees, this may be their only perceived safe opportunity to share their true opinions. In many cases, the survey process is followed by focus groups to gain more insight and clarification, or leadership-led engagement discussions that are used to build trust and understanding and to focus energy with regard to the factors that will help an organization perform better.

Pulse Survey

The second type of survey is the pulse survey. This is a focused survey, usually given to a statistically relevant random subset or cross-section of the organization. In most cases, this type of survey is completed on a monthly or quarterly basis. Organizations utilize pulse surveys to have a basic indicator of engagement throughout the year, provide regular data and a dashboard for executive meetings, raise the engagement issue to a strategic level, and determine whether the organization is making progress on its engagement goals.

Organizations generally utilize one of two types of pulse surveys:

- General progress pulse
- Initiative progress pulse

A general engagement pulse has a subset of items deemed most important by the organization. These may be the items that have the most impact, or they may be items that the organization has chosen to focus on for the year. Regardless of the exact items chosen, there are usually a maximum of ten to fifteen items on a pulse survey, and this type of survey allows the management team to get a quick read on either the current state of affairs or the progress made on certain engagement areas.

An initiative progress pulse is built based on the action planning resulting from the original organizational engagement survey. These items measure the stated goals and initiatives that came out of the action planning process and tend to be very specific outcome-based or action-based items. A survey of this type might include items like the following:

- My manager has held a retention discussion with me this quarter.
- Human resources has provided me an overview of my benefits and compensation this year.
- I have been able to attend a minimum of four hours of training this quarter.

When we carefully measure employee engagement and analyze the results, we can gain a clear focus for our time and resources. As an organization, we can pick the two to three most leveragable areas on which to concentrate. The ability to communicate what those priorities or targets are and why they are important becomes a simpler task, and the organization is able to gain significant transparency. Most importantly, when we are clear on the results, we are able to start action planning and create a more open dialogue with our employees that will lead to real and positive change, as long as we can respond productively to their feedback. After all, we should not confuse measurement with follow-up and building trust.

Questions to Ask Yourself

- What process does your organization use to create your priorities?
- How do you determine the engagement type on which you should focus?
- How does your organization determine impact?
- How is your engagement process tied to profitability, revenue, and/or customer loyalty?
- What analysis does your organization complete on the results?
- What type of engagement survey does your organization utilize? Organization, pulse, or both?

4

THANKS FOR THE GIFT

It was just before my child's birthday party and we sat down with him to have a talk. We knew he had grown to an age at which he was past the idea that getting a present was just awesome. We also knew he would not be content playing with the ribbon or paper anymore. He was old enough now that what was in the box mattered! He was also at the age at which he might react or share his feelings about what was in the box. So we had the talk. You know . . . the one to let him know that this is a gift from someone to you, and whether you like the gift or not you want the person to know you appreciate the fact that he or she gave you a gift.

At first he did not really understand the concept. So we asked him to think about it from the other person's perspective. What if he gave the gift and the other person shared his or her displeasure with him? That's when it sank in. The next part of the conversation focused on what he should say or do, because he was not sure. We did not want to encourage him to lie, avoid the person who gave him the gift, or become defensive and uncomfortable. We wanted him to feel comfortable and respect the other person. After a little discussion and some questions, it became very clear to him. He said, "I get it. They went to the trouble to get me a gift and so I should thank them for the gift."

Well, feedback is essentially a gift and should be handled the same way. When we measure and collect data, our employees take a risk, and they are in a sense investing in the organization. This is not a risk taken lightly either. Most employees want to come to work feeling good about what they do and for whom they do it. They want to do a great job. And they want to help the organization move forward, but sometimes do not know how. Sharing this feedback with the organization is one way they can have an impact. We have the ability, as leaders, to promote understanding and curiosity or concern and fear. Even though the feedback is not directed solely at us, such as in a 360-degree feedback tool, our displeasure for the message can come out. It is our responsibility as leaders to manage our reactions. Here is a five-step model for thinking through handling feedback. (See Figure 4.1.)

Figure 4.1 Handling Feedback

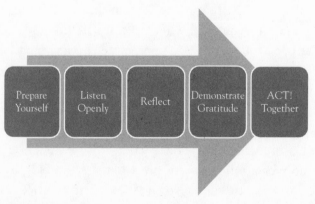

Source: Performancepoint, LLC

Handling Feedback

First and foremost, you should prepare yourself. Be prepared to ask, "What is it they are trying to say?" "Why are they feeling this way?" "What are the implications of the feedback they are sharing?" If you have experienced the organization differently from others, then ask yourself, "Why?" The most important idea is to prepare yourself to be open-minded about the feedback. When you take the next step and hold leadership-led discussions with your employees, listen to them. It is not the time for a debate or to explain why. Hear them out and reflect on what they share with you. This conversation is a crucial moment for you, your organization, and your team. Your employees have given you a gift—the gift of feedback. At this very moment they are questioning what will happen next . . .

- "Will leadership care about what we said?"
- "Are they interested in making changes?"
- "What is really going to change?"
- "Will there be any repercussions because we filled out the survey?"

If this conversation is handled well, you will have gained more momentum in a short time than you could have with a complex and involved intervention. This is a chance to promote trust and collaboration to create the best work environment possible. Dialogue is a powerful tool. Remember, if handled well, it is a two-way street. Your employees should be very involved in the conversation. The most important skills to use will be:

- Asking questions
- Listening
- Tempering your own opinions and agenda
- Managing your own concerns and fears

- Being in the moment
- Being authentic

Take time to reflect on what was shared, including possible solutions. This conversation should be focused on acknowledging where the employees are, but most importantly, where they want to be and how to get there. Above all else, thank them. Thank them for their candor, honesty, and the strength to help the team and organization move forward.

Tips to Remember Regarding Feedback

- Once you ask for feedback, employees expect positive change.
- Ignoring feedback will decrease the engagement of your employees.
- Neither accept feedback completely nor denounce it completely; find the balance.
- If you want a change, you must believe in it.
- Perception is reality. Others will see the organization differently than we do.
- To change the view of our employees, we must first make changes in our organization and in ourselves.
- To truly accept the feedback, you must analyze the data. Think, think, think!
- Watch yourself. We tend to focus on the negative.
- Leverage your organization's strengths. They can be most helpful.
- If you look hard enough, you will usually find themes or patterns in the feedback.
- Recent events can color the data, such as a layoff, stock price fluctuations, or a merger.
- Involve others. Share with others. Get help from others. It helps create success.

We find that the data collected can be spliced demographically, providing multiple types of responses:

- Top down
- Location
- Function/department
- Human resources
- Local leadership
- Age, gender, tenure, minority status, and so forth

Engagement Conversations

It is critical that organizational feedback flow from the CEO all the way to the employees on the shop floor or in the field and back. Not only does this promote transparency and trust, but it fosters dialogue and conversation at the local level on how individuals and teams can improve employee engagement. Discussions regarding data collected can be handled using internal leadership, human resources, or focus groups using outside facilitators. We suggest that the decision on how these conversations take place and who leads them should depend on the current state in the organization. The more trust exists, the more likely it is that you should allow managers of functions, groups, and locations to facilitate these follow-up conversations. After all, the benefit to having a survey is the dialogue and understanding that come from the process. Too many organizations have a few people sit behind closed doors and complete the action planning. When action planning occurs in this manner, there is little to no buy-in.

If the engagement and trust levels are low, we suggest getting outside help for holding these conversations in order to create an environment for productive focus groups and the development of strong action plans. The most important outcome from these conversations is that the employees learn about the

Figure 4.2 Follow-Up Engagement Conversations

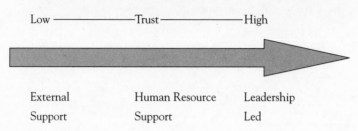

Low ——————Trust——————High

External   Human Resource   Leadership
Support   Support   Led

Source: Performancepoint, LLC

results and have an opportunity to talk openly about them. If the employees do not feel safe, then there is no point in having the conversations. When trust levels are average, that usually means certain areas have less trust than others or certain managers have earned less trust than others. In cases such as these, we encourage a strong human resources team to team up with certain managers to ensure a more positive outcome. The long-term goal, however, is to create the level of trust and skill to allow these conversations to take place with key leaders and their staff. (See Figure 4.2 for an overview of this concept.)

There are a number of agendas one could utilize to hold an engagement conversation. We offer the following agenda as an option or starting place:

Engagement Conversation Agenda

1. Thank everyone for participating. Let them know that their participation and candor are very valuable.
2. Explain the purpose of the meeting.
3. Create ground rules to ensure a safe environment.
4. Review the data.
5. Ask for clarification regarding the feedback.
6. Explore the reasons "why" these challenges and successes are happening.

7. Brainstorm alternative solutions.

8. Explore a specific idea and course of action.

9. Create a plan.

10. Execute the plan.

11. Communicate and celebrate progress.

One suggestion we make to clients is to split the conversation into two meetings. The first meeting should be utilized to share the results and gain clarification. This way we demonstrate the value of the feedback and the desire to understand the feedback prior to taking action. An agenda for this meeting might look like this:

Engagement Conversation Agenda: Meeting 1 of 2

1. Thank everyone for participating. Let them know that their participation and candor are very valuable.

2. Explain the purpose of the meeting.

3. Create ground rules to ensure a safe environment.

4. Review the data.

5. Ask for clarification regarding the feedback.

Planning for this meeting is essential. Otherwise, it can become directionless, or worse, a complaint session. Most important, the meeting should be balanced and focused. We suggest that, while you will provide an overview to the entire set of results, you should be prepared to do two things:

- Share a balanced picture of both the strengths and weaknesses of the organization, department, office, or the relevant breakdown of the results, and
- Know the items that will have the largest impact and prepare to spend time on those.

Figure 4.3 Sharing the Data

	Strengths	Improvement Areas
Items: 1 2 3		
Comments: 1 2 3		
Clarifications: 1 2 3		

Source: Performancepoint, LLC

We have included a chart below that may help you organize your thoughts regarding where you will want to spend your time in this conversation. You will notice that the chart in Figure 4.3 encourages you to think of specifics and to focus on strengths first. It is all too easy to become critical and want to fix what is broken. However, we should always look at what we can celebrate and leverage to create a balanced picture.

Action Planning

The second meeting becomes more of an action planning meeting. This discussion centers on understanding the causes of low scores and working toward solutions. We encourage our clients to keep the action planning simple to make sure initiatives are executed and executed well and to focus on a maximum of three goals and initiatives for the same reasons. It is simply too easy to sit in a room and plan. The difficult work starts when we actually have to make things happen. A potential agenda for this meeting might look something like this:

Engagement Conversation Agenda: Meeting 2 of 2

1. Explore the reasons "why" these challenges and successes are happening.
2. Brainstorm alternative solutions.
3. Explore a specific idea and course of action.
4. Create a plan with milestones, accountability, and opportunities to celebrate and recognize.

It is important to note that this meeting is all about moving forward. It is not uncommon and very helpful to summarize the results of the first meeting and provide the goals for this meeting in writing in advance. This will give participants the opportunity to prepare their thoughts and add more value to the meeting. It is not enough to determine goals. We should be clear on what progress or success looks like. We have included a chart in Figure 4.4 to help you organize your thoughts and action steps.

TIPS for Creating Successful Engagement Conversations

- Use the SMART goal-setting process
  - Specific
  - Measurable
  - Attainable
  - Relevant
  - Time Bound
- Try not to ask leading questions when talking with employees.
- Temper your own agenda. Remember this is not about you; it is about the team or organization.

Figure 4.4 Action Planning

ISSUE	ACTIONS	OWNER	MILESTONE DATES	SUCCESS CRITERIA

Source: Performancepoint, LLC

- The more you ask of others, the more they will bring. They will help if they are asked to rise to the occasion.

- Make sure to work on and spend time on issues that are within your control. Talk about issues that exist in your department, division, or group. If we take this approach we are able to help shift our work environments. Spending time on things that are out of our control typically reduces morale and productivity.

Tips for Celebrating Successes

- Remember to acknowledge efforts in moving forward and successes along the way. In today's busy world, we typically acknowledge what goes wrong rather than what goes right.

- People want to be a part of success and winning. Progress is success and we have a responsibility to shed light on that progress both publicly and privately.

- Here are some ways in which you can celebrate successes:
  - Send notes to individuals.
  - Send out a public email.

- Have the president or CEO congratulate a group for great work.
- Buy lunch or pizza for the group.
- Have a party.
- Have a make your own sundae break.
- Set up game time to let off some steam.

Tips for Identifying Success

1. *Identify your milestones.* What are the key signposts for projects? When is it important to regroup? When does the initiative move into a new phase?

2. *Determine lead indicators.* What are the early sign of success? What activities lead to key results? What does progress look like along the way?

3. *Determine lag indicators.* What end results are we looking for? What does success look like? How will we know we have made the progress we were looking for?

4. *Ask everyone involved what success looks like along the way.* If your people are involved, they will have buy-in. Create a shared sense of success through your conversation.

5. *Measure your efforts along the way!* Defining success is not enough. What should we put in place to measure success? How can we keep this initiative front and center? What structure can we use to keep us all accountable for success?

Tips for Communicating Results

- Communicate, communicate, and communicate!!! The more the better. Repetition is okay.
- People erase emails before reading them and, yes, sometimes by accident. They miss conference calls. They are distracted by deadlines and personal issues during conversations. They miss the details. That does not mean that people's intentions

are bad. They are trying, and like all of us, have much too much on their plates.

- Use different vehicles to update everyone, including emails, conference calls, wikis, intranets, company meetings, and other means.
- Think about how you communicate. We must get people's attention and mindshare. Dry, formal language only serves to reduce comprehension.
- Communicate, the *What's In It For Me,* in each message.
- Be creative:
  - Try using a banner.
  - Make the communication an event.
  - Create a contest whereby people can win if they identify certain things in the message.
  - Create a worksheet that they can fill in along the way.
- Make sure the headline in an email or memo is attention-getting.
- Illustrate how the information in this message helps them, the organization, the team.
- Quick updates are much better than long messages, reports, or meetings, so be concise.

Good luck and enjoy the chance to truly connect with your employees. People tend to think the action plans and the data are the pot of gold at the end of the rainbow, but it is the ability to connect with your colleagues that is the real treasure. The data and the action planning provide a reason and a structure for that conversation and connection. That is why feedback is a gift. Remember, dialogue leads to trust and trust leads to common ground and common ground leads to achievement.

Questions to Ask Yourself

- To what extent does your organization and its management acknowledge employee feedback?

- To what extent does your organization and its management visibly demonstrate appreciation of employee feedback?

- How does your organization currently create a dialogue with its employees?

- To what extent can you and other management take in the feedback and work with employees in a non-defensive manner?

- How does your organization involve employees in the employee engagement improvement process?

- To what extent has your organization utilized focus groups?

- How does your organization define what is worked on locally versus globally?

- How does your organization communicate progress on employee engagement goals?

- How does your organization promote the idea of celebrating successes?

- What process does your organization utilize to determine who leads the engagement conversations?

- What process does your organization utilize to determine whether the engagement conversations are successful?

5

IT BOILS DOWN TO TWO THINGS

In This Chapter

▶ Trust

▶ Distractions

▶ Ego

▶ Agendas

▶ Success

I was recently mediating a situation between two individuals. It was a very difficult situation because the problem had been going on for a long time, approximately fourteen months. These two individuals were fairly senior in the organization. However, their relationship was in turmoil. These two executives were acting like children, and it became such an issue that the human resource group asked for help. Unfortunately, they waited a little too long. I am not exaggerating when I say that it would have been difficult for the situation to have been worse. The only thing these two people had not done is resort to hitting each other, although some threatening language had been used. One of the executives actually oriented one of his new employees by sharing negative information about the other executive, coaching them about what to look for, and then asking the employee to sit in on meetings as a witness.

There were two reasons why this effort was going to be a challenge at best. The first reason was a lack of trust. So much time had passed, with conflicts occurring without resolution or even understanding. Each of these individuals needed answers about what was going on. And true to form, both of the individuals made sense of these conflicts from his own point of view. To create meaning, they had to make many assumptions and fill in the blanks that existed. They chose this path rather than listening to each other and trying to see things from the other person's perspective. Amazingly, human nature generally shows that under stress and in ambiguous situations, we fill in the blanks incorrectly or exaggerate; usually toward the negative. In every situation, these individuals infused negative motives on the other person and provided opinions as facts to support their perspective. They also saw themselves as innocent and did not seem to take responsibility. After fourteen months of this self-indulgent behavior, it is easy to see how they could not trust each other. Each saw the other person as a caricature, a villain if you will. And they saw themselves as saints. Their own self-interest was a barrier to building a relationship with the other person.

Self-interest was not the only reason why this was such a difficult situation. We should ask why they had never worked through these issues. Why did they let this go so far? Why did the organization as a whole allow this to keep festering? What prompted these problems in the first place?

A number of factors had an impact. Politics, reporting structure, geographic distance, dissimilar professional perspectives, different personality type, and differences in communication style all played a role. But they created a bigger issue . . . fear. Yes, the four-letter word. Each of these individuals was fearful of something. One of them was new to the company and the role. This person had a lot riding on their entrance into the company and wanted everything to go perfectly as planned. The other individual, who had just been told he were now reporting to the first individual, felt as though he was losing freedom, and that his relationship with the president of the company was being affected. This individual saw his career being impacted by a new player and wanted to be viewed as he was previously. Both individuals acted out of fear or risk rather than opportunity.

The further down the road they went, more was at stake, especially when each painted the other individual as the villain and himself as a saint. If they were to resolve this conflict, both of them would have to acknowledge their own challenges and faults. Fear can became a larger obstacle when trying to resolve a problem. This was added to the concerns that already existed. Because the situation had gone on so long and had become very public, they knew people were watching, including the president. While we would like to believe that this would create the proper pressure to work through the issues, it actually creates the need for some people to protect themselves.

Unfortunately, that is what occurred in this situation. One of the individuals rose to the occasion and the other individual engaged in self-protection, negative attacks, and breaking agreements. The irony is that this individual was afraid of looking bad, and in the end he lost the respect of a number of people because of that behavior. If the two of them had resolved the conflict, they would have improved their image in the organization, their relationship with the president, and positively impacted their careers and the organization. So this situation boiled down to two core issues:

- Lack of trust
- Focusing on risks rather than opportunities

Employee engagement is no different. It boils down to the same two items. How are our organizational levers or drivers creating more trust? And how are we building an organization where it is easier to focus on success and opportunity? To further understand these two principles, let's define them. (See Figure 5.1.)

Figure 5.1 Trust

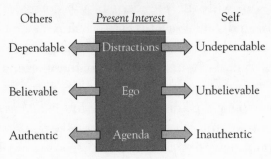

Source: Performancepoint, LLC

Trust

Trust has to do with our present interest. The question we should consistently ask ourselves, whatever the situation, is: "What is my present interest?" If my present interest is truly in others, meaning the person in front of me, my team, and my customers, then I will create more trust. The opposite is also true. If my focus is on myself, self-interest then reduces trust levels. Think of it as a continuum. The more self-interested we are, the more our relationships will suffer or be superficial. This is due to the fact that we cannot focus on other people and their needs when we are focused on ourselves. We just cannot be in two places at once. The challenge we face is that most of us are naturally self-interested; it is human nature. We start our thinking based on where we are emotionally and intellectually. This is most likely due to the way we are wired, but also because of upbringing. From an early age, we are rewarded and recognized for personal achievement. Think back to grade school or kindergarten; when we did something right we received a gold star. When we got the first gold stars, we wanted more. This continues as we get older, only the stakes get higher.

Our training, organizational culture, and work/life style encourage behavior that can be self-promoting or indulgent.

We are not socialized to promote others and think about others before ourselves. Trust impacts our relationships with our supervisors, teams, co-workers, customers, and organizations as a whole. The more trust we have, the more we are seen, individually and collectively, as being dependable, believable, and authentic or real. We want people to count on us, to see us as credible and as straight shooters.

One of our main challenges as human beings is that we are linear, and we cannot help but think about what has previously happened and what will happen. The only problem is that it means we are not in the here and now. When we are in one conversation, we may be thinking about another that has already passed. Or we may be in a meeting and contemplating the meeting with our boss that will occur in the afternoon. Either way, we are not there in the moment.

> *"Be present. I would encourage you with my heart-just to be present. Be present and open to the moment that is unfolding before you. Because, ultimately, your life is made up of moments. So don't miss them by being lost in the past or anticipating the future."*[1]

I was impressed by the quote from Jessica Lange in the above extract. She says it so eloquently. We are either connected to those around us—our co-workers, customers, and employees—or we are not. We have a choice as to whether we will be present and in the now.[2] It is a matter of training our brain to operate in that manner. So what stops us from being present and focusing on others, besides being hardwired that way? What should we look out for to try and keep this in check? There are three factors at the core of this challenge, especially at work—Distractions, Ego, and Agendas.

Distractions

Distractions are everywhere. The sound your computer makes when an email arrives. The buzz of your PDA when it is set to vibrate. The argument with your spouse you had before coming to work. A big football game you want to watch even though you have a project due. Whatever the distraction, when we are thinking about something else or someone else when we are in front of another person(s) or trying to think critically, we handicap ourselves. We will miss details in a conversation, not realize there is a new deadline, or worse, send a message to someone because of the way we are acting that makes the person feel not valued.

I am coaching an executive who is a big multi-tasker. She is interrupted by her staff a great deal during the day. When she is interrupted, it is usually for a good reason; however, she is also focused on other things. She knew that she was not giving her staff the attention they needed, but she would usually recognize it as an issue after the fact; sometimes out of self-awareness, because of a sarcastic comment from a colleague, or because she was surprised by something that was supposedly already discussed. I asked her to think about times when she handled the interruptions well—when her staff felt more valued. I then asked her to think about what was different in those situations.

Her answer was interesting. She said, "The table. I sit with them at a table in the office rather than staying at my desk." It became clear that when she sat at the table in her office she maintained eye contact, did not look at her emails or her phone when calls came in, was able to leave the task she was working on behind, and could focus on the other person. Now she and her staff use a code word to determine whether a conversation can be had at that moment—"tabletop." If she knows it is a tabletop discussion rather than a quick yes or no that is needed, she will either go to the table or schedule time for a discussion at the table later. Here are some tips for handling distractions:

- Schedule time with people when you can concentrate.
- Admit you are distracted.
- Take a walk with that person to change environments.
- Limit checking voicemail and email. Try three to four times a day.
- Exercise or meditate to relieve stress.
- Schedule limits to time spent working on or thinking about particular subjects or projects.
- Organize so you can regroup more easily when you need to come back to a particular issue.
- Manage interruptions. Try scheduled office hours.
- Create words that have special meaning to you and your colleagues to help you focus (like "tabletop").
- Try having people who need your attention triage their questions into categories like "time sensitive" versus "can be scheduled."
- Ask yourself questions to get back to the present moment like:
  - Who is with me?
  - What do they need?
  - What do I hear them saying?
  - Why are we talking?

Ego

Ego is a loaded word, so let's take a moment and expand the definition. For our purposes, ego means focusing on how something impacts you personally and then acting on the basis of that impact. We make decisions every day based on our egos. People decide which projects to volunteer for based on how visible they will be in the company. Ideas, innovations, and best practices are all ego-driven. I know I have never met anyone who wasn't attached to his or her own ideas. Having an ego is not a bad thing. It is only destructive when your ego hampers your ability to listen and understand others and to be present in the moment.

One of the best ego examples I can think of deals with an exercise I do to encourage people to listen, ask questions, and be present in the moment. I ask participants to help me solve a problem in my life. Specifically, I tell them that my wife and I are thinking about having another child, but are unable to make the decision. I then ask them to help me think through this decision. What generally happens is that, rather than helping me to think through the situation, I receive free advice or opinions disguised as questions. The conversation becomes more about the participants than about me, even though I am the one with the challenge.

Here are some tips for managing your ego:

- Keep a journal to become aware. Track the times when you take other people's wins, ideas, or thoughts and make them about yourself.

- Try to analyze your behavior, not just the behavior, but the motive. Are you doing it for someone else or for yourself?

- Be aware of the context. Are you vying for a promotion, wanting a special assignment, or do you want to impress your new boss?

- Ask for feedback. Taking a 360-degree evaluation can sometimes uncover this type of behavior.

- Identify the best salesperson, customer service agent, leader, mentor, or coach and try to emulate the behavior that makes the person successful at what he or she does. Typically, people who excel in these roles manage their egos well when it comes to those they serve.

- Find a coach, mentor, or trusted advisor. They can help you work through these issues.

- Use open-ended, non-leading questions when talking with people and trying to learn more.
- Help others come up with ideas rather than coming up with them yourself.
- Build off another person's idea rather than focusing on yours.
- Try to get in a curious mindset. Ask "Why?" if not to the person in front of you, then at least to yourself.
- Avoid making assumptions.

Agendas

Many of us are structured in the way we work. Some of us think in a linear or logic-oriented fashion. Most of us believe there is a right way and wrong way to approach certain tasks and situations. All of these things represent "agendas." An agenda is a preset approach to something. We have agendas for meetings. A project plan can also be viewed as an agenda. Sometimes an agenda can be a goal, as when a salesperson meets with a client to sell something. Consultants walk into meetings with agendas, such as establishing credibility or adding value to the meeting. There is nothing wrong with having agendas. These approaches, goals, and tools help us create structure and process and serve as plans—a directional compass if you will. The predicament arises when the agenda becomes rigid, inflexible, or the overriding concern.

I had a consultant ask me for help once. He explained to me that he was having trouble adding value in his consultations. He was prepared, flexible with the agenda, participative with his approach, but still had difficulty synthesizing client thoughts and ideas and helping them get to a better place or challenge their thinking. I asked him to think back to his last two consultations and reflect on what he was thinking at those times. He said, "That is easy. I kept repeating in my head, 'How can I add value? How can I add value?'" I told him maybe that was his problem. He asked me what I meant. After a short discussion he had an "aha" moment. He realized that he was so busy thinking about adding value that he was no longer focused on his client. Adding value was his agenda and it was very different from what his customer was thinking about. Once he was able to turn off that voice in his head and become really curious about his clients, he began adding real value in his consultations. Some tips for moderating your agenda follow:

- Ask others for input on any real agenda, process, or plan.
- Walk into situations planning to be willing to change your plan.
- Role play a situation to become more comfortable and natural with it.
- Reverse role play a situation to gain perspective about how a customer, boss, or colleague feels or what he or she wants.
- Watch the repeating. Any time you find yourself sounding like a broken record, there is probably an agenda in there somewhere.
- Pay attention to your internal talk. What are you saying in your head? Usually, when we have an increase in internal talk, it is self-oriented and has to do with ego, agendas, or fear.
- Think about a time when you were curious and had no agenda. Remember what that was like, how it felt, and what was different.
- Actually sit on your agenda, or sit on your hands. It is a very symbolic gesture and it will make you more self-aware.
- Rephrase and confirm what the other person was saying.

Our structures, processes, compensation, policies, and skill sets all impact how much trust exists in our organizations. If we are able to take care of the basic needs of our employees, create a transparent organization, send consistent messages, promote learning that helps individuals become more curious of others and areas out of their expertise, and build a vision that helps people connect to something larger than themselves, we will be more successful and have more engaged employees. Our challenge as organizations and individuals in organizations is to create this work environment in difficult times as well as in optimistic times. Unfortunately, in challenging moments we hold back information, fail to address our motivations, try to put our best face forward, become rigid, or focus on the minutia. All of those behaviors, or manifestations of those behaviors, create questions in our employees' minds. Questions can reduce trust, and the best way we can counter that is to be as straightforward as possible. I used to have a manager who said, "They don't have to like it, just understand it," when he had to deliver less than attractive news. But he was right. Being candid, up-front, and clear went a long way. He also had to deliver the message in a "real" manner. Too many times, people try to oversell something. We all remember the phrase, "If you put lipstick on a pig, it is still a pig."

Questions to Ask Yourself

- What kind of culture have we built, self-interested or interested in others?
- How interested in our employees are we?
- What distractions exist in our workplace?
- To what extent do our policies demonstrate trust in our employees?
- How transparent is our organization?
- To what extent do we practice open book management?
- How political is our environment?

- How do we promote being present and in the moment?
- To what extent does our organization help employees learn to manage their egos?
- To what extent does our organization help employees become more flexible?

Success

Everyone wants to be a part of a winning team. But what makes up a winning team? Success has to do with our present motives. The question we should consistently ask ourselves in different situations is, "What is my present motive?" If my present motive is centered on "opportunity," meaning I am focused on what is possible, then I will create more success. The opposite is also true. If my focus is on risk, then I am trying to reduce my liabilities and will create less success or achievement. We know that this, too, is a continuum. The less we are able to work through our fears, the more likely we will be unsuccessful. There are two reasons for this phenomenon. The first is based on the concept that we cannot focus on opportunities when we are too worried about risk. The second is that if we act on our fear, the very thing we fear most will come true. (See Figure 5.2 for a Success model.)

Figure 5.2 Success

Opportunity	*Motive*	Risk
Perceptive	Fear	Inattentive
Creative	Apprehension	Unimaginative
Accountable	Concern	Unaccountable

Source: Performancepoint, LLC

A wonderful example of the success phenomenon is when a child is trying to learn how to write or read, but juxtaposes the effort against looking good in front of his or her parents. When the need for approval from parents looms heavy in their minds, many children actually become defensive when receiving feedback or have tantrums to avoid doing the work. Amazingly enough, they are so worried about looking foolish in front of their parents that they engage in behavior that not only stops them from learning, but also disappoints their parents along the way.

We see it at work as well. The employee who does not want to upset the boss with bad news, so he procrastinates in telling the boss bad news, only to blindside the boss in the process. The very thing the employee was concerned about actually occurs, and at a heightened level. Also, an opportunity was lost. What if the boss had received the information earlier? What could he or she have done with the information? How could the boss have changed plans? Prepared? Perhaps even benefited from the news? The sad aspect of fear is that it stops us in our tracks. When we are afraid, we are unable to learn, pay attention, or be perceptive to the environment around us, and we are definitely not accountable or responsible for our actions, let alone the consequences of our actions. Most importantly, our clients or customers lose.

On the contrary, when we see opportunity, we are able to do almost anything. The following quote from a commencement speech at Harvard University sums it up better than I ever could:

"By any conventional measure, a mere seven years after my graduation day, I had failed on an epic scale. An exceptionally short-lived marriage had imploded, and I was jobless, a lone parent and as poor as it is possible to be . . . without being homeless. The fears my parents had for me, and that I had

had for myself, had both come to pass, and by every usual standard, I was the biggest failure I knew. . . . I was set free, because my greatest fear had already been realized, and I was still alive, and I still had my daughter whom I adored, and an old typewriter and a big idea. And so rock bottom became the solid foundation on which I built my life."

That quote is from J.K. Rowling, the author of the Harry Potter series.[3] Her success came from no longer having fear. She saw nothing but an opportunity. How do we create an environment in which people do not have to hit rock bottom to see opportunities and where they do not have to be paralyzed by the fear of failure? What if your organization helped its employees understand how to manage fear and conflict so that they were more equipped to act in ways that more consistently create success? Look at your organization and think about the structures, systems, policies, processes, and skill sets that exist. What helps to diminish fear, risk, and concerns of your employees, and what fuels the fire?

Everyone has fears and concerns. Some of us are just better at dealing with them than others. For purposes of this book, I am not going to make a distinction among fears, apprehension,

---

Questions to Ask Yourself

- Have you ever been in a meeting when a colleague picked up on subtle cues you did not even see?
- When have you noticed someone who always seem to come up with a creative solution to a problem?
- How about a leader that took credit for failures and gave credit to the team when he or she won?

or concerns. The reality is that an apprehension for one maybe a fear to another. For practical purposes, what matters is how we respond to fears, apprehension, and concerns. So from this point on, I will just use the term "fear." Fear can cause us to behave in ways that are detrimental to our organization, teams, customers, and ourselves. Here are some examples of how fear can play out in the workplace:

- Tendency to procrastinate;
- Fail to ask our boss or the client an important question;
- Do not call someone back;
- Try to keep a low profile at networking events;
- Act defensively;
- Agree to a request or plan when we are not comfortable;
- Decide not to ask the client for a referral;
- Experience inability to go to sleep;
- Rely too much on policies and procedures;
- Blame others for our inadequacies;
- Avoid an assignment that would help us develop;
- Take on an assignment or responsibility for which we are not ready; or
- Hire people who are not as talented as we are.

If fear is that destructive and is very much alive and well in our workplace and in society, how do we work through fear? There are a number of ways to begin to work on this challenge. I have included just a few ideas to support your growth or the growth of someone in your organization:

- Take a course or read about emotional intelligence or maturity.
- Keep a journal and identify when you stopped yourself from doing something that you should have done or did not

notice or did something that you later realized you should not have. It doesn't matter if it was that you chose not to raise an issue at a meeting, procrastinated on a project, or realized that you were not aware of another person's feelings. Find out why.

- Admit your concerns and fears to yourself.

- Admit your concerns and fears to others. (If it is not a safe environment for doing so, find a confidant.)

- Pay attention to your language. Whenever we use language like "I should have," "I can't help it," "I would have," "I have to," our radar should go up. These are cues that we are being less accountable than we should be, less resourceful than we should be, and we are definitely not going to be perceptive when we are in that mindset.

- Change your language and use language that is more confidant and positive such as "I am client-centered" or "I am willing to share my opinions freely."

- Use visualization exercises. Visualize what you want to happen. Pay attention to what occurred and write down what steps or actions you took to be confident, successful, creative, and/or accountable.

- Find someone who has gotten past his or her fear or is able to do what you have apprehensions about. Interview the person find out how he or she did it. Ask the person to mentor you.

- Make a commitment to someone. When we are accountable to someone else, we are more likely to move forward.

- Break down the problem or concern into smaller pieces so that it is easier to tackle and you can think more creatively about it.

- Identify multiple options to overcome your concern and pick one or more creative new alternatives out of the options you have already identified.

- Think about doing exactly what you are concerned with, and identify the worst thing that could happen and then the best result. Then look at acting in your more comfortable manner and do the same exercise. Compare both sets of results.
- Ask yourself questions such as these:
  - What does being confident or resourceful look like in this situation?
  - What behavior would I need to adopt to accomplish this?
  - What resources and information do I need to accomplish this?
  - How often would I need to do this?
  - Whose support do I need to make this change?
  - How will I know I am making progress?
  - How will I know I am successful?
  - What will be my reward for succeeding?
- Take an assessment that deals with risks and learn more about your concerns.
- Ask yourself "Why?" when you reacted in a manner that is less than confidant or accountable. Try using this as a way to identify your core feelings or beliefs.
- Study personal change by changing small things and getting used to change in general. Then over time up the odds and change larger things in your life. It is a great way to develop flexibility over time.
- Give yourself permission to fail at something. Once you have failed at something and you realize the world did not end, taking risks gets easier.

Trust and success can be applied at an organizational level. Earlier, we discussed "core" engagement factors and "enriching" engagement factors. The concepts of "trust" and "success" can be viewed through that lens as well. Certain factors drive trust and success at a core level, meaning they help me do the basics in my job. Because of these factors I can do my job. Then there are factors that drive trust and success at an enriching level. These factors promote the idea that I am able to do more than a good job. I am gaining a benefit by helping to build something larger than myself. It may be the larger-than-life vision of a company; it may be the idea of social change, or growing a team of people. What it is does not really matter. What matters is that I connect to something at an enriching level. And I can only make that connection if I am able to focus my interest on others and I am acutely aware of the opportunities before me.

The largest challenge organizations have with building cultures of trust and success, beyond the old idea of command and control, is not having all of their ducks in a row. It is easy in this fast-paced world to get out of alignment. We have a tendency to change policies, procedures, and structures in a piecemeal or a compartmentalized manner. Over time, we end up with policies that, at least on the surface, seem to contradict one another, or departments that function differently from one another when it comes to selling or servicing customers. Sometimes, we leave things in place because of politics or sacred cows, even if they no longer make sense. Or we espouse one thing as a part of our culture, and circumstances push us to act differently.

One of my clients was dealing with that very issue. They spoke of trust and belief in their employees. It was plastered on their walls, taught in their training courses, and repeated by senior management. However, on a day-to-day basis there was little to no ability for employees to plan, make decisions, or innovate. It was a "command-and-control" structure. One of the reasons the company was functioning as a command-and-control organization was a deep-rooted need to focus on financials; to try minimizing the risk of poor performance. Unfortunately, the mixed message between the espoused and the real created a great deal of mistrust, anger, and fear and negatively impacted their financials.

In many cases, organizations have difficulty aligning themselves. When you are in the middle of the muck, it is hard to see the forest for the trees. The results are mixed messages and inconsistency at best, something we have termed as "noise." Noise is the result of inconsistent messages being sent in an organization. Organizations that have a good deal of noise, especially during periods of change, create an environment that reduces the amount of trust between functions, levels, and individuals and hinders achievement. Other by-products of noise include the lack of collaboration and innovation.

Organizations can reduce "noise" by holding an audit that reviews their policies, procedures, and systems as to how well they foster trust and achievement with their customers and then with their employees. One more aspect of the audit exercise is how well policies, procedures, systems, and human resource practices of an organization support the organization's stated values. It means that as an organization we need to be honest about our present interest and present motive regarding key policies, procedures, systems, and communications. If we are instituting a new policy regarding vacation pay to save the company money, then we should be honest about it. Employees become frustrated when those decisions are dressed up as a present or as a benefit to them, when they know the organization is acting in its own self-interest.

Another example is non-compete agreements. Too many organizations give the lawyers too much rope. Lawyers are hard-wired and trained to think about risks, so they write a non-compete agreement that is twenty to thirty pages long, covers every "what if" in existence, only protects the organization, and is so stringent it probably won't even hold up in court. The agreement is written in legalize and in effect handcuffs the employees, in many cases, from making a living even if they are laid off from the company. Some of these agreements are written like a long list of threats.

What is the result? I can tell you from personal experience and from coaching people who have also been through this experience. It can take a loyal corporate citizen and turn him or her into a mercenary. I have seen great employees quit; or stay on and then leave to challenge the agreement. I have seen employees hold back their best ideas as an act of revenge. I have seen people become uncomfortable in their office environments because they have seen their employer's true colors. I have seen employees leave and determine how, without getting in legal troubles, they will initiate a direct offensive on their previous employer's business. Imagine you are an employee of twenty years receiving a document like that. It does not illicit much trust or success. It does the exact opposite. Those types of actions cause friction and fear, create attrition, reduce productivity, and negatively impact the financial health of an organization.

Another strategy in addressing noise is to find ways to communicate directly with your employees. Too many companies have chosen static approaches to communication, such as newsletters and email. Other companies rely on confidential questions and answers between the CEO and the employee population. Even others utilize a chain of command to spread messages. Each of these strategies, especially when used alone or relied on heavily, can become ineffective, because they are static and not typically live or face-to-face—and because they invite several versions of a message as it is filtered through the organization.

If we are to live up to our values and support our mangers in creating an engaged culture, we must make sure that every part of our organization is in alignment and communicating the same message. We will need to ensure that each aspect of our organization promotes to our employees a sense of safety, with accountability, and a sense of confidence that the organization has the employee's best interests in mind. We need an environment that allows employees to take reasonable risks rather than focusing on mitigating them. Trust and success are built and earned not only with individual actions, but by organizational mindsets that are communicated through the company's systems, policies and procedures, and human resource practices. Have you earned the trust and success of your employees? To what extent are you focused on trust and success? To find out, take our trust and success profile in Exhibit 5.1.

Answer the following questions honestly using the rating scale below. No one will see the answers but you.

Exhibit 5.1 Trust and Success Profile*

Rating Scale

1 = Never 2 = Seldom 3 = Sometimes 4 = Often 5 = Regularly

1. I worry about the safety of my job/career

2. I multi-task at work

3. I am apprehensive when it comes to trusting people

4. I have been known to hold grudges

5. I spend time thinking about what my boss thinks of me

6. I regret actions or comments I have made at work

7. I feel resentful of others' success or attention at times

8. I zone out during meetings or conversations

9. My credibility or expertise has been questioned

10. I have procrastinated on projects, work or responding to people

11. I have difficulty making decisions

12. People have questioned whether they can depend on me

13. I have difficulty saying things in a clear, concise, and compelling manner

14. I have been seen as having an agenda

15. I am personally uneasy in certain work or social settings

16. I am uncomfortable admitting my mistakes

17. People think I have an ego or need to be smart

18. I am not willing to allow myself to make mistakes

19. I am concerned with what people think of me

20. I keep my feelings inside

21. I am perceived as being negative or holding on to the status quo

22. I feel the need to control things

23. I relate most things to myself or my situation

24. It is important for things to be predictable

25. I have been known to place the blame on others when things do not work out right

26. I have trouble expressing regrets

27. Introducing myself to someone new can be stressful

28. I worry about embarrassing myself in certain social situations

29. I have used sarcasm or destructive comments in professional conversations

30. I am afraid to fail

Scoring

Add the number of points you gave yourself on the assessment. Interpret the results according to the list below.

42 or less   *Engager*–I am able to stay present. I am interested in others and focused on opportunity. I am accountable for my actions and their outcomes.

43 to 66   *Trusted Colleague*–Generally, I can focus others and can manage my fears. I am accountable for my actions.

67 to 93   *Satisfier*–Sometimes I get focused on myself and need permission before I can move forward. I may multi-task too much at times.

94 to 121   *Pretender*–I try to act like I am an engager, but I am really concerned with risks and how I look.

122 to 150   *Victim*–I have a difficult time taking responsibility for things. I concerned with the potential repercussions of my actions.

Questions to Ask Yourself

- How does our culture reduce employee apprehensions about speaking up?
- To what extent are people accountable for their actions and the outcomes from those actions?
- How bureaucratic and policy driven is our organization?
- How resourceful and creative are we at solving problems, especially customer problems?
- What more accurately describes our culture: participative or top-down?
- What are the consequences of making a mistake at our organization?
- What do our policies, compensation, and HR practices illicit from employees? Confidence and openness or protectiveness and concern?
- How one-sided are our policies, procedures, systems, communications, and human resource practices?
- To what extent are our policies, procedures, and systems communicated in a way that reflects an interest in our employees and customers, as opposed to just protecting the organization?
- How risk-oriented is our organization?

Section Two

ENGAGEMENT APPLICATIONS

6

THEY LOST THE GAME ON TURNOVERS

We can all remember the day when a key employee decided to leave. We can remember it because it had an impact on us. When good people leave, we hear about all kinds of repercussions:

- "Our workload increased and became intolerable."
- "Our team was unable to make key deadlines."
- "We had to work fifteen-hour days just to barely keep up."
- "Other departments are bad mouthing our responsiveness."
- "My employees began to question my ability to lead the group and integrity."

Figure 6.1 Turnover Quadrant Model

	Voluntary	Involuntary
More than one year	Career Development	Performance Management
Less than one year	Organization/ Job Fit	Selection

Source: Performancepoint, LLC

Turnover

Turnover also has a significant impact on us personally and on the financials of an organization. According to the Saratoga Institute, the average cost of turnover is one times a person's annual salary.[1] Now, not all turnover is bad. Sometimes, turnover cannot be helped, as in the case of a move due to changes in a spouse's career. In other cases, we may feel we made a poor hire and we want the individual to turn over. But in the end, if we are doing all of the right things, we want to limit turnover, or at least influence it. If our goal is to reduce turnover of key people, we must recognize that turnover is an indicator of a number of issues, shown in Figure 6.1.

Figure 6.1, the Turnover Quadrant Model, is a simple way to review your turnover statistics. The model has two axes. The first refers to *when* actual turnover takes place, wither within the first year of employment or after the first year. The horizontal axis reflects whether the turnover is voluntary or involuntary. When I use the term "voluntary," I mean the person decided to leave on his or her own. When I use the term "involuntary," the implication is that the organization asked the individual to leave. In the next sections, we'll look at the four quadrants of the model.

Turnover Matrix

Voluntary, After One Year

When employees decide to leave after the first year, it is typically because they do not see a career path for themselves. Employees want to be developed and they also want to know there are growth opportunities and a future ahead for them. If they do not see the possibilities or believe that the organization and manager are not thinking about what is next for them, then they have little reason to stay. Instead, these employees use the next job for movement and a guaranteed career progression.

Another reason employees leave after the first year is due to a forced progression. We have all heard the phrases "churn and burn" or "up or out." This language is used to reflect a culture that typically has a pyramid structure with a lot of entry-level people at the bottom and a limited number of more expensive positions toward the top. While this approach is most commonly seen in consulting firms, law firms, and public accounting firms, it is utilized in all industries. There are distinct challenges with this approach and many of the organizations that professed its value in the past have changed their perspective over the years. When you hold this business model and philosophy, people who are very talented and good at their specialty are forced into leadership and/or sales positions. Many of these talented employees are frustrated in their new roles, have difficulty in those roles, or both. Those employees who keep their passion and desire to maintain the skills for their craft decide to leave, and the organization suffers because of the loss, as seen in Figure 6.2.

This career development approach was very common in the 1990s for consulting firms in my industry. Many organizations lost institutional memory, creativity, and intellectual capital because of this model. Firms started to change the model when they noticed the impact on their client relationships and the business as a whole. Most individuals who chose to leave did so

Figure 6.2 Up-or-Out Career Development

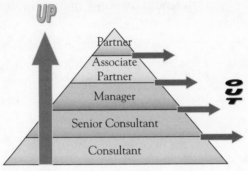

Source: Performancepoint, LLC

at critical career path transitions. Again, I want to stress that this is *voluntary* turnover, meaning that these employees choose to leave and are not "counseled out"—a common term for being asked to leave, but making it look voluntary to save face. We will explore this later. A number of organizations with an up-or-out strategy have active campus recruiting machines. Those firms that have decided that talent trumps the pyramidal structure have had to adopt a more balanced recruiting effort that allows these organizations to recruit and hire what many firms now call "experienced hires."

Career development challenges can also occur because we do not invest in a technical track. While the up-or-out strategy encourages movement up the pyramid or out of the organization whether it is desired or not, there are a great number of organizations that tout the idea that technical, industry, or professional experience is important, but do not reward that same experience. In most organizations, management-level positions are paid at a premium, compared to technical positions, and technical careers can plateau much earlier than management careers. Those individuals who stay at an organization and want to focus on technical expertise, innovation, and being a product or idea leader, as opposed to a people leader, can become frustrated watching colleagues surpass them in status, compensation, and opportunities. What makes this situation even more frustrating is that in many cases these technical positions can add as much or more to the bottom line than some management or executive positions. Some of our clients have moved to a two-tiered career ladder that demonstrates a commitment to both technical and managerial careers to compensate for this challenge.

Many smaller firms or organizations that have stagnant growth become challenged providing career opportunities because employees see little opportunity for movement and advancement in their careers. This can become devastating for an organization, especially when their talent is well-sought-after. Employees are more apt these days to change jobs, roles, and careers and so they look for organizations that can provide opportunities for advancement. Some of our clients in this situation have begun to work on rotational programs and cross-training programs in order to provide opportunities, challenges, and marketability to their employees.

The most common reason employees leave because of career development issues is due to poor practices at their existing employers. Some organizations make the process a paper exercise, forgetting that filling out a form does not challenge an employee. Others create so much bureaucracy around changing roles that it is honestly easier to leave the organization and then come back in the role you wanted in the first place. Part of the problem revolves around whether an organization is inherently interested in developing employees. When an organization takes development seriously, managers are not able to hold employees back solely for their own convenience. I cannot stress how many times I have been told by managers that they cannot let an employee take a transfer or promotion because they needed the person in their department right where he or she is currently. Organizations that truly believe in career development invest in training their managers to grow their people, and they train their employees to grow themselves. However, the key ingredient to creating an environment that "lives" career development is to allow individuals the time to reflect on their careers and to encourage time for managers and employees to dialogue. It is important to make this a this systematic, throughout the organization. Many organizations focus on new people or "early career" employees, forgetting about employees who have been with the organization for a while. Unfortunately, in this way organizations can lose great employees through neglect.

One organization we worked with knew they had a problem losing experienced employees because they had built support systems, training, and development for new hires and simply ignored the needs of their more established employees. They had calculated what it was costing them as a firm, and the number was astounding. It was clear that they needed to change, but they were not committed to the change because the cost became viewed as a cost of doing business and it seemed too difficult a challenge to change the organization's model.

Involuntary, After One Year

If a number of employees are asked to leave after the first year or beyond, this usually connotes a problem with the performance management system, unless you have a strategy to hire a great number of people and then weed them out over time. This is a process people call "counseling out," and it is commonly utilized in "up-or-out" environments. While this strategy can work in the short term, most organizations have changed this approach because of the negative impact it has on building and keeping capability over time. It is also a very expensive process to employ that does not take advantage of the more cost-effective and productive selection tools and approaches available to today's employers. Counseling out employees has a significant number of other negative consequences:

- Breeds a great deal of mistrust in the work environment;
- Hinders the supervisor-employee relationship;
- Reduces accountability;

- Creates busy work as a way of "looking good";
- Decreases teamwork;
- Creates unhealthy internal competition;
- Takes the focus off of the client or customer; and
- Increases fear in the workplace.

Assuming that up-and-out is not your strategy, it should not take over a year to remove someone who is not performing. When people are asked to leave one to two years after they start, somewhere along the line the organization has dropped the ball and it is not fair to the individual or to the organization. I realize that many organizations claim difficulty removing poor performers due to legislation, but when documented appropriately and thoroughly, it is possible. This usually comes back to fear and risk, as opposed to doing the right thing. People are kept on in a workplace even when there is a poor fit because:

- Human resources has become to risk-averse;
- A manager has not documented the problem(s);
- A manager avoids the "difficult" conversation with the problem employee;
- The manager promotes the person in order to avoid dealing with the problem;
- The manager transfers the person in order to avoid the problem;
- The manager sends the person to training as if it were a remedial education program, hoping the problem will work or train itself out;
- An organization values seniority over performance;
- People are afraid to share feedback because of an unhealthy culture;
- The manager and/or human resources is afraid to deal with the problem employee because he or she has a connection with a powerful executive in the company; and/or

- The company feels their hands are tied because of a union contract that was poorly negotiated when it comes to dealing with performance issues.

A performance management system works best when we know whether the employee will work out within three to six months of entering the organization or taking on a new role. For some roles, complex positions, for example, you might even go up to the first year. However, most employers know pretty quickly whether an employee can do the job. The real challenge is being able to take that knowledge and turn it into something more useful. Performance management systems typically focus on results that take time to see. When we rely on these lag indicators to make decisions, it causes us to postpone issues with which we need to deal proactively. Take a consultative salesperson, for example. We can evaluate salespeople based on the revenue they have brought in, which typically is at a minimum after only six to nine months in a consultative sales role, depending on the size and type of sale. That is too long a waiting period to determine whether the person will be successful. Their pipelines can be utilized as a way of determining success. How big is the pipeline? How many opportunities are in their pipelines? What is the average size of the opportunity? But it takes a long time to build an established pipeline for a new salesperson, especially in a difficult economy. However, to create a pipeline and establish opportunities, salespeople must engage in activities such as prospecting, attending networking events, and garnering a certain number of face-to-face meetings in a week. If I am aware of a salesperson's activity, I will know whether or not he or she is working appropriately toward establishing a pipeline. With the combination of both activity management and pipeline management, I will be able to target potential red flags and developmental opportunities. For instance, if it generally takes ten phone calls to get one lead and the salesperson has to make twenty calls to get one lead, we will need to look more closely at the salesperson's prospecting efforts. Identifying issues like this can take as little time as a couple of weeks. When you can quickly pinpoint performance issues using a strong performance management process, neither the employee nor the organization is surprised down the road.

Voluntary, Within First Year

When employees decide to leave within the first year, it is usually due to a poor organizational and/or job fit. Now that sounds like the organization made a poor hiring decision. However, this type of turnover is far more reflective of recruiting errors. While these challenges occur during the selection process, they are specifically caused by selling the candidate on the company and job too much and not providing candidates a completely honest and full picture of the role and the company. This is usually occurs because of:

- Pressure to fill a spot;
- A difficult employment market for employers;
- Ego of the hiring manager wanting to impress the candidate;
- Competitive hiring market for employers so they sell the opportunity;
- An employer trying to make up for perceived market inequities such as a lower compensation levels;
- The natural competitive tension of a selection or hiring process;
- An inconsistent process or messaging from the employer; and/or
- A features and benefits war because of multiple offers by different organizations made to a candidate.

When a candidate feels "sold" and/or disillusioned after starting a job, he or she tends not to stay that long. The best way to deal with this issue is to prepare (in advance of the recruiting and hiring process) what messages you want to send to the candidate. When preparing in advance, an organization should share the attractive and not-so-attractive aspects of the workplace and the job. Those individuals who are still interested will not only take the job, but they will stick around.

It is also possible that the recruiting process does not encourage the candidate to take an opportunity to reflect on whether this is a good match for him or her. We have to remember that a selection process is a competitive process and that candidates feel pressure to perform. They also feel pressure to get the position. Sometimes, this pressure will stop candidates from thinking logically about whether the position is a good fit for them. This usually occurs because:

- Candidates are asked questions like "Do you want this job?" or Why do you want this job?" during an actual interview;
- Candidates are only asked to think about what attracted them to this position or company, rather than asking about any concerns as well;
- Candidates are only asked why they liked the job opportunity and not about what they may not like about the opportunity;
- Candidates are pressured to respond and make a decision in the moment or quickly;
- Employers ask the questions and control the process, creating more of a parent-child relationship and causing the candidate to take on a passive role; and/or
- The selection process is viewed as a test by the employer and candidate rather than a mutual information-gathering

and decision-making process, causing the candidate to focus on impressing the company, as opposed to making a good decision.

Because being hired is about "winning" a job, we need to create moments in the hiring process that provide breaks from that need to win and ask the candidate to perform his or her own analysis about whether this is the right move. We can take the view that it is the responsibility of the candidate; however, as employers we are largely in charge of the process—and with that comes responsibility. We also must remember that there is a fiscal benefit for taking responsibility. We can reduce turnover by taking action. Organizations that choose to consistently paint a balanced picture, encourage candidates to determine whether there is a good fit, and provide a structure in which to understand that the role, while a good opportunity, is not perfect, can reduce turnover by an average of 8 percent.[2]

Involuntary, Within First Year

The last quadrant relates to candidates the organization asks to leave to leave within the first year. If this is occurring more than it should, then we are clearly looking at a selection process challenge. This type of turnover points directly to poor decision making. Reviewing your entire selection process, standards, training of interviewers, and so forth would be a recommended approach. Most challenges occur in this quadrant because:

- The organization has not created a clear profile for the position;
- The competencies and skills associated with the position are not clearly defined;
- The selection process is not comprehensive;

- People make decisions without a process, relying on their guts;
- Interviewers are not using behavior-based questions or they use the same questions regardless of the job or role;
- The organization is not using a rating process or the rating process being utilized is not effective;
- Hiring managers compare candidates to each other rather than to the job requirements;
- Decisions are made by someone removed from the work or not inclusive of those involved in recruiting and interviewing;
- Candidates are treated differently or inconsistently in the interview process; and/or
- Hiring managers are not trained or trained correctly on how to interview and use the interview process.

Most of the time, we find that our clients try to do a good job at hiring new employees, but the distractions of everyday work life, the lack of time, and the difficulty preparing all of those involved with selection get in the way. Hiring is more challenging than most people believe. Most of us understand what our organizations are like and feel we are good judges of character, and that feeling can lead to a false sense of self-confidence, especially when we view hiring as a simple process. We see this with clients all of the time. Behavior-based interviewing has become a common term and most organizations feel they have a behavior-based process. However, we have seen that most organizations are not executing the process correctly. Using a behavior-based process is much more complex than asking past event questions, and it is impossible to train managers well in a two-hour module. The turnover quadrant model is not an entirely exhaustive model. It is, however, practical and simple to use.

Using a model such as this is helpful when looking at the entire organization; however, greater insight can occur when analyzing various areas of an organization separately. For instance, if we look at a typical organization's turnover, we may find a mixed set of results. We may find we have work to do in each of the quadrants. Sure there is some insight gained, but we might not have a lot of wisdom and here is why. Certain roles in the organization may have different needs than others. Figure 6.3 is an example.

Many organizations have collections departments or telephone sales departments. Those types of positions can be very challenging because of the conflict or rejection received on a daily basis. When an organization hires to fill these types of positions, it is imperative that they help a candidate understand what the disappointment and rejection feel like before the person accepts a position. If an organization has not instituted this step for these roles, we may see voluntary turnover for such employees in the first year.

On the other hand, we may find that engineers are voluntarily leaving after the first year. This may be due to a career

Figure 6.3 Segmented Turnover Matrix

	Voluntary	Involuntary
More than one year	Engineering	Face-to-Face Sales
Less than one year	Telephone Sales Collections	Administrative

Source: Performancepoint, LLC

development issue. It may be because of a lack of advancement or a lack of exciting, cutting-edge projects. Engineers may leave because they do not feel valued like their managerial counterparts. However, we would not realize this was an issue if we did not break down the turnover in different ways.

If we continue to break down the data, we may find that salespeople are being asked to leave after a year's time, telling us that we have a performance management challenge in that area of the organization. The last quadrant shows that most of the turnover for the administrative positions in this company is occurring within a year and that it is not voluntary. If this were happening in our company, we would know that we need to look at the selection process for administrative positions and make changes accordingly. What if we looked at turnover using other demographic lenses such as gender, minority status, and location? What insights would we find?

Turnover is a central aspect of employee engagement. People who are engaged are nine times more probable to continue with an organization—that is, not leave—than those not engaged.[3] Turnover of an individual can quickly impact a team, division, or even an entire organization. If we think about a company of twelve people, if one person leaves it can be devastating. Even if you consider a large company, most teams are relatively small. The effect of a few people leaving can significantly shift the engagement of others, affecting their ability to meet deadlines and to achieve. Turnover alone is not the issue. After all, we can keep the bodies in the building, even if the souls have left. The larger questions are: "How do we keep the whole person passionate?" "How can we get the person to connect his or her head, heart, and hands to the mission of the organization?" Turnover is just one signal of when and where we may have a problem. Now deciding what we should do about that challenge is where the hard work begins.

Questions to Ask Yourself

- How much turnover?
- Where is our turnover occurring?
- How much does the turnover cost our organization annually?
- To what extent do we embrace a "churn-and-burn" culture?
- To what extent do we embrace an "up-or-out" culture?
- To what extent do we hire and promote from within versus from the outside?
- To what extent have we analyzed our turnover?
- How are technical careers treated versus managerial careers?
- Why do we think the turnover is occurring?
- What can we do about the cause of the turnover?
- How is the turnover impacting others in the team or organization?
- What does our turnover say about our employee engagement needs?
- How many souls have left the building?

7

BRING THEM ON

The Selection Process

A productive selection process is a valid process. Let me define the term "valid" clearly. In the case of a selection, evidence of validity means the selection process demonstrates that it:

- Makes sense to all parties including the candidate;
- Is reflective of the job and the tasks associated with the job;
- Measures content that is reflective of the job;
- Is predictive of success; and
- Measures what it intends to measure.

A strong selection process contributes to decisions, positive or negative, that reflect a candidate's ability to do a job and be productive in the organizational culture. The employment environment has changed in recent years. We now have a number of generational differences at play. Hiring processes must account for the twenty-two-year-old just out of college, to the sixty-year-old not ready to retire. In some cases, we have candidates returning from retirement who want to work again. Younger professionals are typically more comfortable with technology that is utilized in the selection process; while many older candidates may feel put off by a significant use of technology. We also have more competition for good candidates. Many organizations have vacancies open more months at a time. These changes are driving real shifts in the way that we bring people on to our organizations. The efforts that some organizations have made to tie their hiring process to engagement are most interesting. Let's take a look at the difference between a traditional hiring process outlook, and one that is tied to engagement, seen in Figure 7.1.

Hiring used to be thought of as a hoop to jump through or a test, and when we found someone who seemed acceptable; we used a probationary period to ensure we did not make a poor choice. That three-month period was a safe time to reverse the hiring decisions we had made. We thought of candidates as

Figure 7.1 Traditional Hiring Versus Engagement Hiring

Traditional Hiring	Hiring for Engagement
"Let's determine whether they are a good fit in the first three months."	"Let's make sure everyone has an oppportunity to succeed in the first three months."
"Find me a good candidate."	"Let's build a relationship with our candidates."
"This is a test."	"This is a mutual decision."

Source: Performancepoint, LLC

qualified or unqualified, and diligently tried to push that categorization as quickly as possible. Now, organizations are shifting to a more balanced picture. First and foremost, we know that when we create a highly stressful environment in order to qualify people, we reduce the level of trust between the individual and the organization, setting ourselves up for negative branding and poor decisions.

Once, a friend of mine went to an interview and the room was very hot. The interviewer asked her to open the window. When she tried, she was unable to make it budge. As she looked down at the windowsill, she noticed that the window had been nailed shut and covered with paint to make it look like a normal window. She realized that the room, the heat, the window were all part of a setup to see how she would react. Needless to say, she was not happy with these tactics. She thought about her next move and whether the interview even mattered to her anymore. Then she picked up a chair and asked, "How badly do you want this window opened?"

An extreme situation, but illustrative, nonetheless. She no longer trusted that potential employer. The organization also created a situation that would make most normal candidates choose even more carefully what information they would share, or whether they still had an interest in the position. Either way, the potential employer actually limited the amount and/or quality of information it would garner from the interview.

The other factor that comes into play is fear. The more fear or pressure we create in an artificial situation (it will not match the same stress level or type people actually feel on a certain job), the more likely we are not to get a true picture of candidates. They will most likely respond in ways they think will please us or create the least amount of risk. After all, they are competing for a position. Unfortunately, this will tell you very little about how they will behave on a day-to-day basis in the job when their guard is down. No, our goal is to get to know the individuals and have them get to know us. Our goal is not about being touchy-feely. We need to make an educated mutual decision that leads to building a brand and increased odds of success for the individual who takes the position.

There are significant selection and on-boarding differences between employers who have high levels of engagement and those who do not. Take a look at some key results from a Watson Wyatt Study[1] that identified differences in the hiring and on-boarding practices of organizations with high levels of engagement versus those with low levels of engagement (see Figure 7.2).

In highly engaged organizations, hiring managers are trained in the desired way to interview candidates. This is a key challenge because everyone thinks he or she can interview, and yet most people do a poor job of it. There are a number of misconceptions about interviewing, even on widely noted techniques such as behavior-based interviewing. Most people do not know what they do not know. Strong training provides information and knowledge on selection and hiring and also provides ample

Figure 7.2 Low-Engagement Versus High-Engagement Practices

Low Engagement	High Engagement
• 33% provide interview training for managers	• 65% provide interview training for managers
• 29% share with new hires the attributes that drew the company to them—poor financials	• 52% share with new hires the attributes that drew the company to them-high financials
• Spend 1 day to 15 weeks grooming new employees	• Spend 35 weeks grooming new employees

Adapted from Watson Wyatt's 2006/2007 WorkUSA Survey

opportunity to practice skills needed to hire well. A strong training program on hiring should include, at a minimum:

- Hiring philosophy of the organization;
- Costs of poor hiring practices;
- Benefits of productive hiring practices;
- An overview of the selection approach;
- How to prepare for the interview;
- How to define what success looks like in a particular job;
- How to conduct an interview to best predict success;
- How to rate a candidate and make a decision;
- How to make an offer;
- How to onboard a new employee; and
- Legal issues involved in hiring and selection.

If a company decides to utilize other tools such as testing and realistic job previews (topics we will touch on shortly), then even more could be added to the training. What is most striking is that organizations attempt to tackle all of this training in two to four hours. The reality is that there is no time to practice, the session amounts to an information dump, people receive a generic list of questions, and they all have a false sense that they know how to interview well. To practice probing for more information, identifying what is a complete answer, rating correctly, and mastering other essentials of effective interviewing takes time. Typically, an organization can do a good job of training, covering these topics in a day. However, if you want to conduct mock interviews and provide feedback for participants along the way, a day and a half to two days is required.

Second, highly engaged organizations specifically share with the candidates they hire what attracted the company to them. What a simple and practical tool, if used on a consistent basis. It makes the chosen candidate feel good, shapes his or her knowledge of what will help him or her succeed in the new environment, and begins to help the person connect particular talents to the success and strategy of the organization. I read the book in graduate school called *Ropes to Skip and Ropes to Know* that utilized stories to demonstrate the ins and outs of organizational culture. More importantly, these stories helped the reader become aware of the potential pitfalls that exist in organizations and the ways that the readers could use this knowledge to help themselves succeed.

Gaining a clear picture of the candidate during the selection process is important, but doing so in a manner that can be applied to improve the engagement and potential success of a new employee is powerful. How often have we said or heard someone else say in response to the question about a new employee, "What will make them successful and what could hold them back?" "I don't know yet. We will have to give it three to six months to see." Even if we do know the initial (I use the word initial because our assessment will change over time) answer to the question, have we discussed that knowledge or perspective with the new employee?

Last, the on-boarding process is significantly different in highly engaged companies. Highly engaged companies spend approximately thirty-five weeks grooming new employees. This is almost nine months! That is much more than a company orientation; it is an investment, and a significant one at that. How many orientations have you seen that last half a day or just two hours? Many organizations say they have an orientation, but few actually do. Most orientations consist of a human resource paperwork race, some color commentary on the vision and mission of the organization, and a review of key policies and procedures. If an organization does go beyond that effort, it typically includes an introduction to key executives and areas of the organization and a checklist of what should be completed by the employee with the support of the manager. However, rarely are the checklists or follow-up procedures more than a ceremonial effort. Of course, signatures and dates are applied to demonstrate progress, but what accountability really exists? How do we measure whether the efforts created real progress? In what ways do we determine the quality of these efforts?

While a selection process needs to be respectful, it is also important that the selection process be challenging and comprehensive, and that it encourages your candidates to think about the opportunity in front of them. A comprehensive selection process will look at four components that an individual will bring with them to the job (shown in Figure 7.3):

Knowledge: What information, facts, technical background, and data does this individual have as it relates to the position?

Personality: What qualities, style and preferences does this person have that will help them in performing this role?

Motivations: What drives this person and will help them fit in with the company and enjoy working in this role?

Competencies: What skills and abilities does this person have that will help them succeed in this role?

Figure 7.3 Four Components

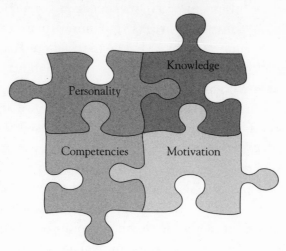

Source: Performancepoint, LLC

If you think about it, we have the answer sheet . . . the job itself. The profile of the position, if defined well, serves as the success measurement when hiring people. When you define the hiring process, you are trying to achieve a vehicle for putting the puzzle together for each candidate. That process takes time. In workshops, I like to ask participants how long it takes them to prepare for an interview with a candidate. The answers range from fifteen minutes to (usually) an hour. Then I ask them to review with me a purchase they have made recently. Typically, people pick things like a flat-screen television. When I ask them how they prepared to make a decision for that purchase, I find that most of the people visited several stores, looked online, purchased *Consumer Reports,* and read the reviews on flat-screen televisions. The time investment to prepare to make a decision before working with a store employee is usually five to forty hours. What is startling is that the cost of an employee is much more significant than a television, and the impact is as well; yet we make an inverse investment of our time with regard to the selection process.

There is no way we can determine those four key components of a job, define the selection process, develop great questions, and ensure good structure in fifteen to twenty minutes. Some organizations try to interview people for half an hour prior to hiring them. How can we even begin to determine how well the candidate compares to our four components that quickly? It would be difficult to successfully achieve the goal in an hour. We also have the added challenge of on-boarding a new employee in a productive manner. If we spend our time on the front-end selection process and we are collecting information about the candidate we hire, we can do a lot more than make a good decision. With good information comes good decision making, good coaching, and good development. Companies that understand this concept are able to help new employees leverage their strengths and minimize any areas that could hinder their success. These companies are able to help an employee and, from day one, create a development plan that encourages growth and connects the employee to the company. This can only be accomplished through an efficient and effective systemic process based on job requirements.

What tools is your organization using or not using in the selection and on-boarding process?. Let's take a look at some of the tools that are available:

Targeted Recruitment Plans

Targeted recruitment plans are created and executed to provide an organization with the most cost-effective recruitment while garnering top-quality candidates. Rather than going to the usual wells that your organization and others have already drained, a targeted recruitment plan seeks to use particular language and knowledge of transferable skill sets to identify new recruiting sources, determine which previous recruiting sources are still relevant, and communicate with each of these sources in the most effective manner.

Assessment Centers

Assessment centers are built to evaluate a job candidate's strengths and weaknesses in relation to a specific job or role, such as the role of an engineer or leader. Customarily, assessment centers have utilized results from multiple evaluations, including intellectual or ability testing, personality assessments, job simulations, role-play activities, and in-basket exercises. These measures are specifically designed for a particular role and managed and administered in a centralized manner and in controlled surroundings. The selection measures are administered by well-trained and qualified specialists and raters. The results, including recommendations, are provided in a specific report by a psychologist or assessment center expert.

Realistic Job Previews

A realistic job preview (RJP) is designed to assist a candidate in determining whether he or she is indeed a good fit with the role in question. RJPs provide a total view of a particular job, including a balanced picture of the advantages and potential disadvantages of the job. When designed well, an RJP involves the candidate in the selection process and has him or her share responsibility for making a productive hiring decision. The idea is that the job candidate, provided with the time, opportunity, and information, can in many cases better decide his or her own appropriateness for the job. This process increases the chance for success and reduces voluntary turnover.

Experience Checklists

An experience checklist is usually a short form filled out by a candidate. The checklist is designed to spotlight attention on pertinent experience to a particular role. An experience checklist assists the decision-maker by saving time and keeping him or her on target. It also aids the job candidate in providing all the germane information.

Pre-Screening Interviews

These are short, structured interviews used to identify essential credentials and competencies. Screening interviews can be conducted face-to-face, by telephone, or by using technology. The entire purpose is to efficiently remove unqualified candidates early in the process, saving time and money.

Personality Assessments

A personality assessment is a questionnaire that can be administered via paper or the web that measures various work-related personality traits that have been shown to lead to success in a particular job. These tests must be designed to hold up under legal scrutiny. To ensure your organization is using an appropriate assessment, have someone review the validation evidence related to the test.

Intellectual/Ability Testing

Certain positions require the ability to do math, move packages of a certain weight, type a certain number of words per minute accurately, or apply abstract thinking. Some hiring processes include one or more intellectual or ability tests. Again, these measures must be connected to the role, have evidence of validity, and be administered consistently and precisely.

Behavior-Based or Structured Interviews

Behavior-based interviews are comprehensive interviews compared to pre-screening interviews. It is typically behavior based, although there are other approaches available, developed to identify specific competencies that are most relevant to the job. This interview guides hiring managers, individuals charged with interviewing, and human resource practitioners to job-related, legally defensible questions in a consistent and effective manner.

Engagement Interviews

The engagement interview measures an individual's past behavior related to developing and maintaining a commitment to his or her work and work environment. Each employee can drive the business forward, manage his or her career, help others to do the same, and do so in a manner that builds a more trusting environment in which more people can achieve. This type of interview allows an organization to measure these things, as well as accountability and ownership.

In order to be successful, organizations may need to explore changing their approach to hiring. They will need to explore new types of structure that create a shared partnership between the candidate and the company. A great term for this is reciprocity, meaning shared dependence, cooperation, or exchange between persons, groups, or states.[2] We need a process that creates a more mutual and even exchange. For instance, an organization may try setting up an interview solely for the candidate to ask questions, as opposed to allowing candidates to ask questions only at the beginning or the end of the interview. Another idea might be to have the candidate come to the interview prepared to interview the hiring manager, alternating so that each person asks questions and receives equal opportunity to learn from the other.

Questions to Ask Yourself

- How does this role impact the success of our organization?
- Do we have a strong profile of the job?

- How are we branding the company when selecting and on-boarding candidates?
- How are we weeding out candidates in a respectful manner?
- To what extent are we sure we are keeping the candidates who are most likely to succeed?
- Have we put our least expensive selection tools up-front?
- How effective is our process?
- What responsibility are we putting on the candidates?
- How does our process build trust with candidates?
- How does our process impact success of new employees?
- How positive are we that we are gathering good quality information about candidates?

On-Boarding

A strong selection process should create trust, maintain the dignity of those involved, and support the organization's on-boarding process. If the selection process was handled well, a new employee should be able to walk into a company with pride and confidence, ready to learn and contribute. An organization should know that the best decision has been made and be armed with knowledge to coach and train the new employee and to reduce the new employee's learning curve.

Imagine having a discussion with a brand new employee and working jointly through:

- Work style and preferences;
- Knowledge related to the job;
- Motivations;
- Strengths; and
- Potential development areas.

Imagine relating this conversation to the position, the team, the organization, and the strategy of the organization. As a new employee, what a "wow" this could be. Add to this a dynamic development process that already identifies as part of the development plan potential available resources such as:

- Activities
- Books
- Tips
- Training

Transition Plan

Once a candidate is on board and you have a good understanding of what he or she brings to your organization and the position, and the candidate does as well, it is important to think about a transition plan. This is more than an orientation or development plan. It is a vehicle for making a mental transition from the old to the new. When someone comes on board, he or she is thinking about past positions or his or her schooling. The new employee has a mental model of an old world that may or may not help him or her in this new environment. How do we create a new picture? How can you help the person understand what that change looks like and feels like? The more concrete and clear the person's picture becomes,, the more likely this individual will succeed. (See Figure 7.4.)

I knew someone who took a new job. He was excellent in his field, had a strong reputation, produced great work, and maintained excellent client relationships. The new job was identical to his role at his previous company. It was a perfect match—or so everyone thought.

While the roles were the same, the companies were not. The new organization was a smaller company with fewer resources. The newer company had been in business a shorter time, and

Figure 7.4 On-Boarding Steps

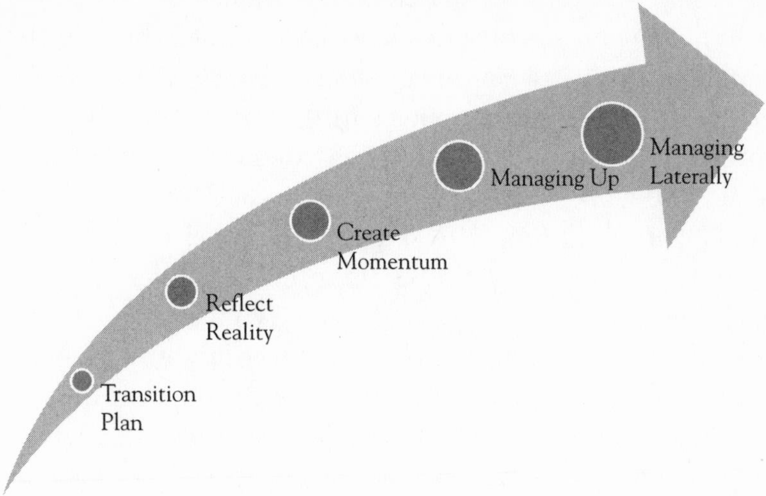

Source: Performancepoint, LLC

products, services, processes, and marketing resources were less developed. Well, my friend was frustrated with the new company and the role. He was overwhelmed and felt as though he was not receiving the appropriate support to be successful. The truth is, it was all about him. He was working in a manner that reflected his mental model of his role at the previous company. He had not clearly identified the differences between work environments, and until he did he was going to feel as if the new company had let him down. He needed a transition plan and the new company should have helped him to build one.

Reflect Reality

The next step in the on-boarding process is to help shorten the learning curve. The best way to speed up someone's transition is to reflect reality. To reduce someone's learning curve, we must go beyond sharing information about his or her strengths and development areas. We must help the person understand the organization, both formally and informally, and how he or she as a new employee fit into the new organization.

What talents do new employees have that will help them succeed in this particular organization? What approaches might they take that will create bumps in the career here? What hot buttons, unspoken rules, and sacred cows exist that employees should know about in order to be successful? We're really asking: "What are the ropes to skip and the ropes to know?" The last aspect of reducing the learning curve relates to sharing the "Why's" and the "How's." Most new employees receive a large number of directions. They are given finite tasks and are asked to shadow people. However, often they have questions regarding why an organization handles things a certain way and how everything fits together across departments. These new employees are usually hesitant to ask and are sometimes even discouraged from asking questions. Not many organizations would purposely discourage questions. Unfortunately, questions can be seen as challenges, and organizations often do expect new employees to earn their stripes prior to challenging the status quo. Time is also a factor. In the heat of the moment, with a number of tasks in front of a manager or another employee, it is easy to shut down the conversation or discourage questions. But that drive to get our tasks completed can send some strong signals to a new employee. Ironically, by not dealing with the "Why's" and the "How's," we lengthen the learning curve and eventually take up more of our own time.

Create Momentum

When an individual joins your organization, how often is he or she successful? We want *every* new employee to be successful. We also know that success breeds success. So we should have a plan, specific assignments, or opportunities for all new employees to create initial successes. What are the early wins we will help them achieve? How can we recognize the small successes?

How will we create momentum? Momentum means a lot, largely because momentum reduces fear, increases comfort, and boosts confidence.

When new employees begin working in a company, they wonder how they are doing. Some new employees worry about whether they are meeting expectations. What better way to send that message than to create early opportunities to achieve. We should not only look at projects but each phase or milestone as an opportunity to let a new employee know how he or she is doing, and if possible to celebrate the person's progress.

Managing Up

Every new employee, even with early wins, is still trying to fit in. It is up to us to help that employee understand how to create productive dialogue with his or her manager. Managers should help new employees understand how they can "manage up" in the organization. They want to know how to manage their relationships with their managers.

Managers who are willing and open to sharing their preferences and creating a safe environment during the on-boarding process make managing up easier. This is the time when employees learn to bring solutions to identified challenges or not to bring solutions because their managers will provide a solution regardless. This is when employees learn whether it is okay to say, "My plate is full" or "If you want me to finish that by tomorrow, which of these other projects are you willing to reprioritize until after?" Employees want to know what they should take on themselves and what they need to run up the flagpole. This is the time to provide that clarity and start to build good habits.

Managing Out

Another key area is managing laterally or "out." New employees, to be successful, must understand how to work with others, specifically colleagues and those in other departments. What does teamwork look like in your organization? How do people work cross-functionally? What does collaboration look like in your workplace? Knowing the answers to these questions can be the difference between success and failure for your new employees.

One of our clients has a sales function. The sales representatives are focused on meeting customer needs and have an incentive to do so. Their partner in meeting those needs is the warehouse and distribution team. Unfortunately, the warehouse team is more focused on predictability regarding hours and wages. There have been times when an order was supposed to be shipped one day, but it would go out a day or two later because it fit the preferences of the warehouse. The only problem was the impact it had on the customer. If you are new and are not aware of the relationship and the challenges between departments in this organization, you could find yourself in an unpleasant situation. Because you are new and lack credibility, the situation could have an unfortunate impact on your career at the company.

An orientation can only begin to scratch the surface on the five on-boarding success factors we have just discussed. An orientation cannot possibly answer all of the questions associated with on-boarding. We must develop on-boarding processes that are defined, managed, and measured. We should ask the important questions and have answers ready for new employees. We can demonstrate to new employees their value and improve their chance of success by setting aside time on a regular basis over the first ninety days to discuss any issues that come up. These efforts take time and cannot be rushed. If they are valued by management, then more employees will be successful.

Companies can build a brand and increase employee engagement through their recruitment, interviewing, testing, and other selection tools. When we view selection as a vehicle to build a brand both internally and externally, to improve the engagement of our employees, and as an important link to on-boarding, we can see that selection is a strategic process. It is imperative

Figure 7.5 Example of Selection On-Boarding Process for a Specific Client and Role

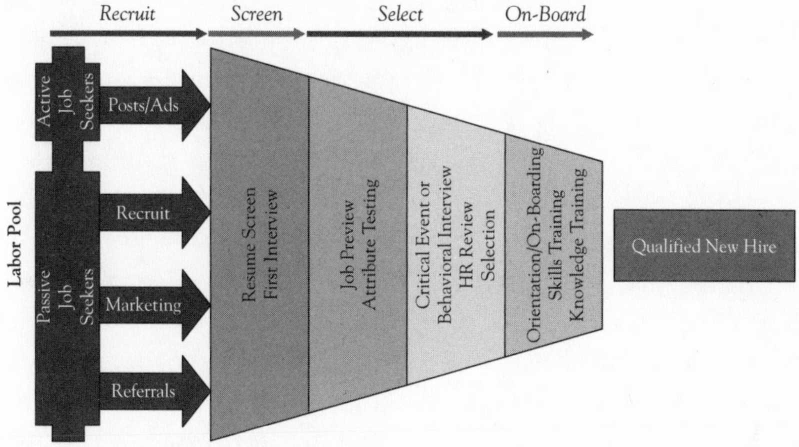

Source: Performancepoint, LLC

that this process drive results, create cost and time efficiencies, and promote good decision making on the part of both the company and job candidates. Let's look at Figure 7.5, which gives some examples and results of the selection process. The following text shows how a client of ours followed the process.

Case Example of a Realistic Job Preview

One of our clients in the media industry, a smaller player, wanted to find a way to demonstrate their commitment to employees when recruiting candidates. We spent time with them rethinking their entire selection process, including the use of selection assessments and having a more structured interviewing approach. However, one decision they made, I believe, best sums up their philosophy and the spirit of their process.

One of the key challenges they face is that they are in an industry that is a magnet for new graduates, students just out of school. The students pose a real challenge—they do not know what they want to do. These students may be interested or even enamored with the industry, but without experience in the industry they do not know what role they want to play. After talking about this challenge, we decided to employ the use of a realistic job preview. This tool usually provides information and/or asks questions that encourage candidates to think about whether the role and the company are a good match for their skills and preferences. Organizations may use a number of mediums to accomplish this task, including video, computers, or paper and pencil.

These are not tests. The answers candidates provide are never shared with the company and do not determine whether or not a candidate gets a job. A realistic job preview provides candidates with a chance to be a part of the selection process. It demonstrates how important it is to the employer that the candidates make the best decision for themselves that they can. Candidates are given time and space to reflect on what they learn about the role and the organization. They are usually encouraged to think through the questions and answer honestly and candidly. After they have finished with the realistic job preview, candidates decide whether they want to continue with the selection process.

This particular realistic job preview actually helped candidates not only determine whether the organization was a good match for them in terms of a place to work, but it also helped them differentiate among the three typical entry-level roles available. If they wanted to proceed, they contacted a human resource professional and shared what they felt would be the best match for them. This tool has

- Improved the perception candidates have had about this organization;
- Allowed candidates to take more ownership in the selection process;
- Improved initial conversations between entry-level candidates and human resources;

- Improved the likelihood that candidates accepting positions will stay;
- Increased the confidence of a new employees that they will succeed and have made a good decision;
- Demonstrated to existing employees the commitment the organization is making to bring in the right people;
- Illustrated to candidates that the organization wants candidates to make the best decision for themselves; and
- Set the organization apart from their competition.

The survey is completed online, but we have included a sample of it in Exhibit 7.1.

Exhibit 7.1 Example of a Realistic Job Preview

Introduction. It is important for you to know that this is not a test. The answers you provide will not determine whether or not you get a job. This is a "realistic job preview. It is meant to provide you with a chance to be a part of the selection process. It is important to us, here at Horizon, that you make the best career decision that you can. By answering the questions on the following page you will be able to determine the position for which you will, most likely, be best suited.

Please answer the questions honestly and candidly. After you have finished, take time to think about your results. When you are ready, please share with your Horizon human resource contact what area of Horizon you feel will be the best match for you. Talk with the person about the reasons why you feel that way. If you utilize this tool correctly, it can help you in making your own job decisions and start you off on a productive career.

Thank you.

Directions: Choose the answer that best fits you.

1. I would rather:
   a. spend time doing project work on the computer
   b. make quick decisions and move on to the next thing
   c. work through a stressful challenge with others productively

2. I feel most comfortable when I:
   a. work with others on a project
   b. ask questions to gain necessary information
   c. have a plan that I can execute

3. I enjoy:
   a. learning new software applications
   b. discovering what others think
   c. developing a routine and discipline

4. It is more important for me to:
   a. work in a good environment with a strong team
   b. decide what to do based on what is right
   c. maintain my composure and demonstrate professionalism to others

5. People say I:
   a. pick up on new technology fairly easily
   b. consider others when I make decisions
   c. manage my time well by focusing on critical tasks

6. One thing I know about myself is that I:
   a. can support the team even when I feel differently
   b. hardly ever procrastinate
   c. remain calm even under difficult circumstances

7. I find I prefer:
   a. variety in the work that I do
   b. an assortment of tasks on my plate
   c. being able to maintain order in my day

8. It is best when I:

    a. use my intuition

    b. analyze data

    c. look at different courses of action

9. I feel I can not compromise my:

    a. ability to be honest and candid

    b. sound judgments based on what is right

    c. respect for others

10. I have been most successful:

    a. working on a team

    b. understanding others' needs

    c. achieving results

Answer Sheet

Write your answers below and total the number of a's, b's, and c's.

1. a. _____   b. _____   c. _____

2. a. _____   b. _____   c. _____

3. a. _____   b. _____   c. _____

4. a. _____   b. _____   c. _____

5. a. _____   b. _____   c. _____

6. a. _____   b. _____   c. _____

7. a. _____   b. _____   c. _____

On Question 7, if you answered "a," also put a "b." If you answered "b," also put an "a." If you answered "c," do not count it.

8. a. _____   b. _____   c. _____

On Question 8, if you answered "b," also put a "c." If you answered "c," also put an "b." If you answered "a," do not count it.

9. a. _____ b. _____ c. _____

On Question 9, if you answered "a," also put a "c." If you
answered "c," also put an "a." If you answered "b," do not
count it.

10. a. _____ b. _____ c. _____

Total: a. _____ **b.** _____ **c.** _____

If you have a higher total of "a's," then you will most likely
prefer a Planning role. If you have a higher total of "b's," then
you will most likely prefer an Account Services role. If you have a
higher total of "c's," then you will most likely prefer a Buying role.

My client succeeded in creating a process that was challenging, made candidates think, improved their decision making,
and still promoted trust and reduced anxiety. Most importantly,
they improved their hiring decisions and on-boarding in the
process. Another example of a different type of a realistic job
preview is a story rather than a survey, shown in Exhibit 7.2.

Exhibit 7.2 Story Example of a Realistic Job Preview

Introduction. It is important for you to know that this is not a
test. The answers you provide here will not determine whether
or not you get a job. This is a "realistic job preview." This instrument is meant to provide you with a chance to be a part of the
selection process. It is important to us, here at TrenchSafety,
that you make the best career decision that you can. By reading the following information about the position and then
answering the questions at the end, you will be able to determine whether this position is appropriate for you.

Please answer the questions honestly and candidly. After
you have finished, take time to think about your results. If you

utilize this tool correctly, it can help you in making your job decisions and start you off on a productive career.

Thank you.

A Day in the Life at TrenchSafety. Pat Jones was one of the most successful sales representatives at TrenchSafety.

Pat worked his way through college as a part-time surveyor and graduated with a degree in civil engineering. After graduation, Pat worked for a regional contractor, but tired of traveling for weeks at a time, so he came to work for TrenchSafety. He always said, "To make it in this business you have to understand construction!" I now know that he meant work in it, get schooled in it, or both.

Pat found out about TrenchSafety from the Internet. He actually spent a fair amount of time researching the industry before applying for a position.

During the interview process, Pat asked many questions. To an outsider, it might have been difficult to determine who was interviewing whom. Curiosity like that is what made him so good at helping customers solve problems.

Pat displayed an unusual thirst for knowledge. Even though Pat participated in TrenchSafety's intensive TrenchMaster training program, Pat wanted to learn more. At night, he took home brochures, books, PowerPoint presentations, OSHA regulations, and other training materials. On some weekends, Pat borrowed equipment to practice demonstrations. He even bought a couple of books on Amazon that he thought would be helpful.

Early in his TrenchSafety career, Pat found a site-prep contractor who let him "shadow" a grading crew for a couple of days, so that he could learn more about moving dirt. He convinced another contractor to let him help lay pipe. He was not afraid to get dirty and was willing to be out in the heat and the cold.

Frankly, at times, Pat was a "pain" because he had so many questions. He was also persistent in asking when he would be qualified to teach a "competent person" class. Nevertheless, that was OK. In the process, Pat mastered the products and mastered his customers' applications.

Pat spent just as much time learning about his sales territory. He took advantage of the tools at TrenchSafety, including the ACT database, trade association publications, D & B, and customer lists. Pat also spent time studying Reed and Dodge data.

Pat developed and committed to writing quarterly, monthly, weekly, and daily plans. In the process, Pat always knew where to go and what to do. He was truly a determined, goal-oriented, self-starter.

Since Pat spent a lot of time in his truck (a 2002 Ford F150 that he bought for $5,000 and rebuilt himself), Pat would analyzed his route to maximize time spent with customers and minimize driving time. Pat also spent time analyzing call frequency and thinking about the best times to see customers. He was aware that time was money for himself and the customer.

Pat utilized TrenchSafety's PipeTrax to track his deals and details about his customers.

When a selection process works, the results can be outstanding, as can be seen in Figure 7.6. One of our clients revamped their entire selection process based on the work we had done with them. The results they achieved were better than expected. In fact, they were able to see fewer people, save time, and make more confident offers to their candidates. But the amazing result had to do with the acceptance of offers. The candidates are challenged, and as a result of the process the percentage of acceptance increased. More candidates wanted to work for this organization because of the way they were treated during the selection process. That success continued after these individuals started working for our client. Their turnover rates decreased and their productivity increased. Selecting the right people the right way makes a difference in the way we commit to our employees and in the way they commit to us.

Figure 7.6 Results

Steps	Traditional Process	Improved Process
Campus Interview	40	20
Office Interview	15	10
Offers Given	7	7
Offers Accepted	4	5.5

Source: Performancepoint, LLC

Questions to Ask Yourself

- How effective is your current on-boarding process?
- To what extent does your on-boarding connect with your hiring process?
- How do you utilize insights gained about the candidate during the hiring process in your on-boarding?
- What type of transition plan exists for a new employee at your organization?
- How does a new employee learn about the culture and norms (especially the informal ones) at your organization?
- To what extent do you help a new employee gain an initial win or wins?
- How does a new employee learn to effectively manage expectations and relationships with his or her boss or senior leadership at your organization?
- How does a new employee learn how to work across department and division boundaries?

8

ENGAGING LEADERS, ENGAGING CULTURES

There is a saying in business, "Leaders cast a long and cascading shadow." It is a rather profound statement. So many executives want to change their organization and its culture, and yet the last place many of them look is at themselves. Most cultural ills of an organization start with the habits, emotional intelligence, and decisions of its key leaders, and this is also where the remedy should begin.

One of my clients has been trying to change the culture of their organization for some time. Periodically, we receive a call from our contacts there, trying to promote a new step they have taken. In the last few years, they have introduced a new set of competencies, a novel cultural statement, a fresh branding approach, and a clean performance management system, among other initiatives. These are all wonderful interventions, and they have not hurt the organization. In fact, these efforts have helped the organization in many ways. The problem is that the organization is not addressing the challenge they have set for themselves. This organization desperately wants their people to take on more responsibility, demonstrate more initiative, and help drive the organization to the next level. Unfortunately, most of the employees share this ideal, but agree it is not the reality.

The executive team can be very controlling and passionate, to the point of overwhelming, and the employees respond in kind. If the organization wants employees who take on real ownership and are innovative problem-solvers, it will need to start with the executive team. This is about higher-level managers, key leaders, creating a culture of trust and achievement, versus one of self-interest and apprehension—a challenge that exists in many organizations. It is about true collaboration.

Collaboration

Psychological Associates utilized a realistic simulation over a four-year period to gain insight as to how executives actually work with employees.[1] Every executive participating in the study had an objective to inform an exceedingly skillful direct report that (s)he was not receiving a much-desired promotion. Additionally, each executive was to share with the employee that, while he or she was qualified for the position, he or she was not receiving the promotion due to his or her people skills or lack thereof. The last objective for the executive involved preserving the direct report's intent to stay with the organization. In the end, each executive was to make sure that the direct report was aware that he or she had future prospects at the company.

The research pointed to the need for collaboration and involvement when working with employees, especially during conflict. What was so surprising was that, contrary to the research, executives made the choice to utilize communication techniques that allowed them to maintain firm control of the discussion, and that created a parent-child dynamic with the employees. Here are some key results from the study:

- Twelve percent of the executives checked to see whether the direct report was able to continue the discussion.
- Seventeen percent asked the employee's thoughts regarding the employee's action plan.
- Sixteen percent of executives tested for understanding in the discussion when it came to the different views presented.

Most of the meetings were spent using statements, closed questions, and communication designed to structure the meeting. One of the clear results was that many executives lacked the very same people skills they were discussing with the direct reports.

We at Performancepoint completed a survey of over four hundred professionals.[2] We found the number-one concern from employees had to do with "trust in senior leadership." When we delved in to the qualitative answers, we found very similar responses. Executives communicated with employees in ways that were perceived as controlling and parental, especially under difficult circumstances. Many employees questioned the sincerity of key leaders in their companies, largely because the employees did not feel as though they were treated as trusted professionals and adults.

We recently embarked on an additional survey, and the preliminary results indicate that the factor perceived as most significant with regard to long-term productivity and intent to stay is "senior leadership," and the largest frustration employees currently have is the lack of direction from senior leadership.[3] There are numerous examples in today's workplace that reinforce this issue.

Awareness vs. Adoption

Clearly our emphasis on employee engagement has not created the behavior change we are looking for in our organizations. We may understand what impacts employee engagement, we may use feedback tools and promote appropriate behavior, but that does not mean that the behaviors we stress will be adopted on a day-to-day basis.

Much of the work in the performance improvement arena with regard to leadership has been awareness-driven. We utilize surveys, feedback mechanisms, and development plans to promote self-awareness among leaders and executives. We focus on creating more alignment between the executive's self-views and other people's views, including direct reports, peers, stakeholders, and customers. However, awareness does not necessarily translate to adoption, and these programs generally fall short on execution.

To adopt new skills, we must change behavior. Personal behavior change is a difficult process, sometimes met with resistance, and for many it can be an emotional undertaking with false starts and relapses. Most importantly, changing behavior takes time. Fortunately or unfortunately, when a leader takes a 360-degree feedback tool and becomes aware of his or her challenges, there are high expectations that change is coming. When a leader is unable to translate that awareness into real actions, employee engagement is reduced.

On-the-Job Training

One of the best ways that people learn is through on-the-job training, right? Most of the research I have seen actually shows mixed results. Sometimes on-the-job training works, and other times it falls short. This inconsistency could be explained by personal preferences in learning, and this probably does play a role. However, we tend to forget that a great deal of learning occurs through self-reflection and our environment or the examples before us.

Self-reflection is not an activity that most of us take on naturally. In fact, because of our schedules, it becomes difficult to take the time. More significant is the inability for many of us to ask the right questions in order to reflect on or to critically and accurately review our approach. Another complication can be the work environment, specifically the examples from which we have learned. How many of us have had the best role models in our careers? How many of us were lucky enough to have a mentor or a coach as a manager from whom we could truly learn?

I was doing some work with a non-profit organization that works with individuals to assist them in saving money, changing their financial habits, and gaining homeownership. When people went through the education process, over and over again, they would remark on never learning the right way to handle money. What was even more powerful was that these individuals knew exactly where their bad habits came from—watching their parents. Until the training opportunity occurred, they thought they were doing everything they were supposed to do. On-the-job training is very much the same, and often our managers can unintentionally help us become misinformed and develop bad habits. Those absorbed habits set the stage for how well you, as a leader, will engage your employees.

Exemptions

In other cases, executives and key leaders are completely exempt from efforts to improve employee engagement. Usually, the reasons have to do with time, creating a separation between one part of the hierarchy and another, or a belief that the efforts are "not for me." In the end, these "reasons" are just excuses. Most often, they reflect the fear of the executive team. In organizations with strong leadership, executives realize the need to start from the top, to stay engaged, and to support the effort as it continues. One of our clients has a CEO who shows up live or via satellite to every leadership session to demonstrate his support, promote his own lessons learned from the program, and begin a collaborative dialogue with his employees. In every leadership development effort I have ever witnessed, whether key leaders participate or not has been a strong determinant to success. When leaders remove themselves from the rest of the organization, they may feel better, but the employees will question them, their actions, and their strategic choices. Unfortunately, these questions are rarely raised out in the open. The questions are shared behind closed doors, over coffee with fellow disenfranchised, and in the soft tone of a whisper; one so soft that most leaders don't hear it.

The Technical Route

Some organizations focus on technical or business acumen skills. They may send leaders to executive programs at colleges or concentrate on simulations that demonstrate the results of certain decisions. These types of development are helpful in a number of ways. They serve up a number of great "aha's" and even intellectual stimulation, but in looking at much of the learning from a safe distance, participants can miss out on real work necessary to improve their leadership capability. What we find with this approach is that leaders are smart. These leaders typically can:

- Analyze a profit-and-loss statement or a balance sheet;
- Understand the textbook answers to business questions;
- Develop broad industry knowledge;
- Develop deep technical knowledge; and
- Think strategically about their businesses.

The challenge these leaders face is being able to manage being "smart" alongside the realities of business. These leaders struggle with the idea that it was easier in class. They are confronted with the reality that accomplishing things in the workplace while being a role model, living up to the values of the organization, growing your employees, and doing all of this collaboratively is very difficult and that their training did not prepare them for the ultimate challenge. We cannot engage others simply by being technically capable. Engagement is about mutually beneficial bonds that drive commitment.

Step-by-Step

Another option many companies take is to provide programs that focus on skill building. Organizations spend a significant amount of money teaching managers and executives the key steps in dealing with employee situations. We put together processes and ask everyone to utilize a particular process when dealing with employees. There are so many mnemonics and steps in an organization at any given time that most people cannot remember them. Most people forget these shortcuts after they return to the real world. If they do utilize these tools, many leaders approach their use in a rote manner. They hold meetings with employees in a structurally correct manner, without real understanding and meaning.

What is most disheartening regarding this type of approach is that it assumes every situation is the same. Step-by-step leadership does not account for the individual differences each of us brings to the table, the differences in various situations, and the relationships that exist or do not exist between employees and leaders. The world is not that linear and predictable, and many of the leaders who use this approach reduce their effectiveness and the engagement of the team around them.

The Art and the Science of Leadership

Leadership can be defined, and guidelines can be provided for various challenges a leader will face, but there is an art to being a leader. The art can be taught, but not in half a day or a day, and not with purely skill-building techniques.

Real leadership is as much an intuitive process as it is skill-based. The very best leaders are able to pick up on subtle cues that other people drop in conversation. They recognize when something is wrong when others are unaware. They carefully and productively pull out the issue hidden under passive aggressive behavior when it is easier to just walk away. When someone is angry with them they become curious as to why, versus becoming defensive. These great leaders manage to self-regulate, keeping an even keel in stressful times. When leaders more consistently behave with presence "in the moment," they are able to promote the collaborative culture for which we strive.

Organizations need a different approach to leadership development, an approach that combines the strengths of what the traditional choices offer. Imagine if our leaders participated in a process that combines a strong leadership model, a realistic and fairly complex simulation, 360-degree feedback or competency assessments, personality or work-style assessments, skill-building and practice, and peer coaching.

To create the culture of an organization that we all desire, we must challenge ourselves in three key areas, shown in Figure 8.1:

- Problem-solving skills;
- Leadership and people skills; and
- Business acumen.

Problem-Solving Skills

Problem-solving skills are essential in today's business environment. We must innovate each and every day at work. Our challenge when training on this subject is to avoid problem solving in a vacuum. Most developmental efforts in which we engage are built solely as an exercise, removed from real challenges and feedback mechanisms in our work environment. In a classroom, the repercussions of solving or not solving a problem just

Figure 8.1 Making Connections in Executive Development

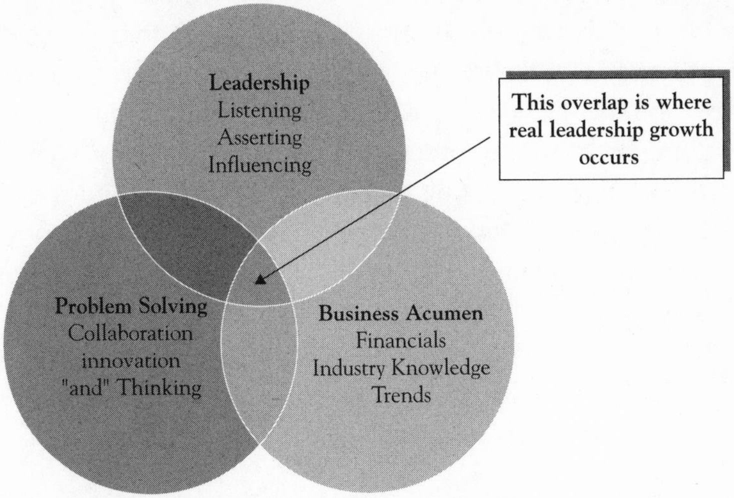

Leadership
Listening
Asserting
Influencing

This overlap is where
real leadership growth
occurs

Problem Solving
Collaboration
innovation
"and" Thinking

Business Acumen
Financials
Industry Knowledge
Trends

Source: Performancepoint, LLC

are not there. We become quite good at solving problems in the classroom; unfortunately, in the real work environment our emotions, stress, responsibilities, demands, and the needs of our employees and co-workers affect our ability to solve problems. Also, most challenges we face in the classroom reflect a focused issue. However, in today's organizational environment, we face complex challenges that cross functions, teams, work groups, and sometimes organizations. Any leadership development program that emphasizes building a common culture must reflect the significant challenges executives face each day.

Earlier, in the Preface to this book, we briefly mentioned the concept of "or" versus "and" choices. How often, in our leadership and culture-building programs, are we pushing our executives to look at their problem-solving behavior patterns? Most of us make decisions in the same way again and again, regardless of the variables involved. Each of us has preferences. Unfortunately, many of us do not recognize or acknowledge that those preferences exist. A preference I have witnessed being manifested in the workplace a great deal is the choice of "right versus wrong," or one choice versus another. It astounds me each time I hear people talk about collaborating, and I watch and I just don't see collaboration. I see negotiation, competition, compromise, avoidance, and accommodation much more often. To collaborate with another individual or team means we must be willing to hear and understand the other point of view, and that person must be willing to hear and understand our point of view. From there, both sides can begin a process of co-discovery. Co-discovery is about building something new and better out of an old set of ideas. Imagine going into a meeting with two very different, possibly opposing ideas and building something more unique, stronger, more interesting, and successful than what you were wedded to when you walked in the door.

Leadership and People Skills

Leadership is the ability to guide, motivate, and influence others over a sustained period of time and in different types of environments and conditions.

Think about that definition for a moment. Charisma is not in there. "Guide," "motivate," and "influence" are behavioral and measurable. Real leaders can repeat their success because they are flexible and understand that different situations and people need different things. They balance the use of tools they have in their toolkits such as listening, asserting, and influencing in a manner that allows others to be heard and still move the organization forward. They are able to incorporate others' ideas and build something better because they utilize disagreements as an avenue for solutions. These leaders hold people accountable, are firm, and yet still come across as inclusive.

When we develop our executives, we discuss issues, topics, and situations they may encounter as leaders. But how often do we challenge our leaders under situations that cause them to question what should take precedence? When we lack time, confidentiality ties our hands, challenging news awaits us, or we are faced with the potential choice of business survival versus caring for our employees, what do we do in the moment? That is the true test of a leader. Most of our development does not take into account these types of parameters.

Leadership is not simplistic. It is not easy. It is one of the most difficult skill sets and abilities to develop. One of the people I respected from afar was Tim Russert. He seemed to understand what it meant to truly be present and in the moment, to be curious about others, to admit and talk through others' fears, and, most importantly to help others do the same. Mr. Russert was known for his authenticity. After he passed, I was heartened to hear so many people say that the man we watched on television was the same person off-camera. He was considered to be the very best at what he did by individuals on the left and on the right. Now that's an accomplishment.

Another challenge our leaders face occurs when business circumstances seem to conflict with the values of the culture. Think about a time when your organization faced a real challenge or crisis. Now think about the values for which your organization supposedly stood. How did your organization meet that crisis? Were you able to handle the crisis in a way that respected each and every one of your employees and your customers? Leadership during great times is riding the tide. True leadership emerges when it is really needed during those difficult or uncertain moments.

Business Acumen

Business acumen is the art of examining the external landscape, understanding how your business connects to it, and quickly making profitable decisions, changes in course, and strategic commitments based on that knowledge. This ability can be the differentiator for organizations. Certain executives are natural at this. They seem to see patterns and connections where others do not. These executives are steps ahead. This ability can be developed.

But again, it is rarely developed alongside problem-solving skills and leadership. The combination of these competencies is powerful. After all, if you can see the future and no one will follow, what is the point?

Most business acumen development focuses on understanding financials, broadening industry knowledge, exploring future trends, and economic and political implications. Each of these areas is extremely important, but the challenge is working through these issues in front of your employees while collaborating with them.

It is the connections among these three competencies that create real challenge. There are times when they feel at odds, when we feel significant pressure, when the situation is ambiguous at best. It is exactly at those times when we realize what kind of leaders we are. Most of us fall prey to our comfort zone when we are stressed. If we do not practice, build up the necessary habit structure, and create development opportunities that mimic our significant challenges and all the complexity that comes with them, we will revert to our comfortable habits. If we are unable to draw on each area appropriately, we limit ourselves and our ability to help create organizational success.

Unfortunately, many organizations have fallen prey to choosing a safe training environment versus a challenging one. If your organization is one of these, I challenge you to do both. Two trends I have seen in recent years stop us from creating this type of learning environment. The first is the *need for the silver bullet*. Many organizations, like people, want instant gratification. We want the ultimate solution, and we as service providers have been keen to say we have found it. In the service provider's defense, many of us are passionate about what we do. We are believers because there are a number of solutions that can have an impact. But making a difference may require an approach that is not easy and that takes more work than we expect. Another trend I have witnessed in the workplace is *defensiveness* and/or unwillingness by some to look at themselves or their organizations realistically. All of us want to be successful and feel good about who we are and what we do. We should be able to feel good about ourselves and still be self-aware. We should be able to acknowledge shortcomings and work toward being more perfect people. While we will never get there, we should still try. Otherwise, we are hiding our heads in the sand.

Two great ideas for addressing these concerns have come from the field of leadership and organization development:

- *Appreciative Inquiry:* The focus on positive change. This discipline is about exploring and investigating organizational life from a positive perspective. When an organization needs to embark on a new strategy. those who practice this discipline look to the organization's strengths as vehicles to achieve success.

- *Strength-Focused Development:* This approach is similar to appreciative inquiry, but used for people development. The idea is that we gain traction when we focus on growing our strengths and we lose traction when we focus on developmental needs.

Both of these ideas are powerful and helpful. They are also a response to the history of our field. We used to look for the "very best way" to do a particular task and then we forced everyone to complete the task the so-called "right way." Then we acknowledged that there existed multiple ways to approach work and that it was important to allow people to approach their work in the way they felt comfortable. We began to focus more on "results." We have now moved into the realm of focusing on *strengths.* If we leverage our strengths, we should be able to produce better results. People should actually choose work roles based on strengths. Now that sounds pretty good!

However, if we juxtapose these two approaches against the two trends I mentioned above, they can be construed as an excuse for not performing or not changing. I have seen people turn down developmental assignments because they did not feel they related to their strengths. I have seen people passed over for assignments and promotions because the strengths identified with the titles listed on their cubicles (which are now labels) are not perceived to be the right fit for the role. I have seen organizations run aground because the world around them changed, and the senior team would not take a critical look at their business. In a great economy, we have the luxury to focus only on strengths. Many businesses succeed in spite of themselves during good times.

For example, one medical company we worked with was growing at a fairly good clip. They had convinced themselves they were successful at sales and as a business. Anyone looking at their numbers would agree. However, they were in a growth market due to the aging population and the increase in the average lifespan. If they were not growing, that would mean they were doing everything wrong. The bigger questions we should ask ourselves include:

- What is our growth rate as compared to the market growth rate?
- What is our growth rate compared to our competitors' growth rate?
- What would our growth look like if the market was flat or shrinking?
- How prepared are we to compete for market share if there is a shift in the market?

During difficult times, change is not always positive or comfortable. There are times when it is difficult to build from strengths. The world is changing faster and faster. There are times when we do need to re-create ourselves or our organizations. We must look at both our strengths and our developmental areas. The pendulum, for many, has swung too far. We used to look for what was wrong, and now most of us look for what is right.

Either way, we only see half of the picture. We need to see both clearly and then make conscious decisions.

One example of how we view development is in our language. Language is symbolic. It tells us a great deal about our values and beliefs. We have changed the words we use for development over time. Early in my career, people used the words "strengths" and "weaknesses." Then there was a time when the preference was to use the words "strengths" and "challenges." The next version to come out was "strengths" and "development areas." Now we say, "What are your strengths and development areas, and please focus on your strengths."

Fundamentally these ideas do makes sense, but if you combine them with many people's tendencies, they can be abused. Developmentally, we need to think more like the boxer with an impressive southpaw or the switch hitter in baseball. In orchestrating sustainable results, you are your organization; your preference might be to play the clarinet, but if the flutist is ill and you can play the flute, then why not fill in? You are a more valuable player, and the performance can continue. Everyone benefits. This stance in no way means to ignore your passions, skill sets, or strengths. Just see the entire picture, be flexible, and know that everyone has the capability to learn, grow, and change.

Being comfortable means that you may be standing still while the rest of the world is moving. Focusing solely on your strengths can be a way to maintain comfort that is a recipe for decline. We need to ask ourselves how we can create a developmental environment that is safe, challenging, and a bit uncomfortable, especially for our leaders. To truly impact engagement in a sustainable way, our leaders must proactively build the culture they desire, and they must model effective growth and development.

Building a culture is not an event. Training alone will not create a culture. Development can create a shared language and a base of understanding. Building a culture is a process. An organization must hold its leaders accountable, clearly articulate values, and manage by those values.

Questions to Ask Yourself

- How do we set the tone in our organization in a meaningful way?

- What is our process for creating a culture and environment in which people support each other and maintain accountability, real responsibility, and trust?

- To what extent do we challenge our executives to explore leadership, problem solving, and business acumen as they are intertwined?

- How are we creating a collaborative versus a controlling environment?

- How do we create daily innovation?

- How can we achieve our goals and still live our stated values?

9

HOW MUCH CAN YOU BENCH?

As the economic environment becomes increasingly complex, moves faster, and encompasses more change, organizations encounter new difficulties. Most organizations have reacted to these challenges by reducing bureaucracy, improving efficiency, and expecting more from employees. Employers desire stronger contribution from employees—especially new leaders, because they have a significant impact on the engagement of others.

Unfortunately, while change occurs quickly, individuals take a longer time to adjust. We have all witnessed new leaders, once

Table 9.1 Differences Between Individual Contributors and Leaders

Individual Contributor	Leader/Coach
Exhibits technical competence and develops credibility and reputation for strong work	Displays a broad understanding of the business and/or technical areas
Able to work independently and create results	Motivates others, utilizing ideas and knowledge
Takes accountability for a clear piece of a project or segment of work	Takes accountability for entire process, area, etc., without control
Works well with direct colleagues	Develops a strong internal and external network
Needs less supervision and starts to develop oneself	Grows, develops, and influences others

Source: Performancepoint, LLC

praised for their success, who suddenly lose their luster. Why? The shift from an individual contributor to a leader is a tricky one.

Career Transitions

Webster's *New World Dictionary* defines "transition" as "a passing from one condition, form, stage, activity, place, etc. to another."[1] In essence, a transition is a significant shift. The most significant shift in the workplace tends to be when an employee is moving into his or her first leadership role. In fact, studies have confirmed this concern. New leaders can fail up to 50 percent of the time.[2] That is an astounding number! The reason this particular transition is the most difficult has to do with the fact that everything a person has learned thus far in his or her career can actually cause him or her to fail in the new role. Table 9.1 shows some differences between individual contributors and leaders.

The challenge of assuming leadership can be one of the most detrimental challenges an organization faces. Leadership at all levels must be strong; otherwise, corporate messages are misunderstood, employees are demotivated, and we create bottlenecks that severely handicap productivity. A client of mine faces this very problem. They have managers in place who are not leaders. These individuals function as individual contributors with authority over people and teams. Many struggle in working across boundaries and departments in the organization. They have quickly lost respect from their peers and direct reports. Projects have stalled in this environment, and client needs have been neglected. Most interestingly, these non-leaders have allowed others to refuse to work together on anything. In the end, nobody wins. I recently asked my contact in the organization, "What do you do to identify potential leadership, prepare those people for leadership positions, assess whether individuals are ready for leadership positions, and transition those individuals who are ready into leadership positions?" Her answer was: "Not enough." We must deal with issues way beyond skill changes, incorporating transitions such as those shown in Table 9.2.

When we first shift to being supervisors or managers, our compensation changes and usually includes an risk component (bonus) based on the accomplishments of a team or department. This shift alone can make some people uncomfortable because they now have less control over their compensation. For many managers, having a portion of their pay contingent on others or performance outcomes may be relatively new and disconcerting. However, that is only the beginning. They also have a loss of control as it relates to workload. Previous to being promoted

Table 9.2 Individual Contributor to Leadership Transition

Area	Individual Contributor	Leader/Coach
Compensation	Individual performance	Team or organization
Control	Significant	Little
Recognition	Great deal	Little to none
People skills	Some	Significant

Source: Performancepoint, LLC

to a supervisory role, employees on a team are completing individual work tasks. As employees, we have control of our choices and the pace of our work. As new supervisors, we no longer have that control. We are responsible for a set of shift, team, or department outcomes. We could supervise three people or twenty-five people. Regardless of the number, as new supervisors we are now judged on other people's accomplishments. Because we cannot control people, we have to learn to influence others.

The next significant change is that we are no longer the STAR players. We are now the coaches. When everything goes well, our people are recognized (hopefully by the boss), and when things do not go well we will need to take the responsibility. Another major transition is the shift from interacting with a limited number of people in certain types of situations as needed, to spending a larger amount of time interacting with all sorts of people in various situations as a means to get things done. Our people skills must rise to the role. To transition to the role of supervisor, developing our flexible communication skills will become paramount. Looking at each of these factors, it is no longer a surprise why moving into a leadership role is a challenge. To successfully transition, a person must overcome past habits and preferences; deal with stress and emotions, and develop a brand new mindset. To assist individuals in this transition, employers must understand why we fill positions with individuals that are not ready.

Causes of New Leader Failure

Typically, organizations have a sink-or-swim mentality, and so a great number of new supervisors struggle or fail. Unfortunately, we're doing a disservice to our employees and teams, the organization as a whole, and that promising individual who has taken on an assignment that is way above his or her head. So why does this happen? Two core reasons for this problem are described below.

Open Spaces Needing Faces

Organizations struggle to find people with the skills necessary to do jobs. Positions remain open for months at a time. And pressure builds in the organization to fill spaces with faces. But after a period of time when someone who is not qualified to fill the role is in it, an organization feels more pain than when the position was open. Our need to fill vacancies by lowering standards, changing job profiles to make it easier to find a candidate, or making exceptions for specific people causes part of this problem.

Moving On Up

The other reason organizations experience pain during leadership transitions is due to the need to get ahead. Individuals are intent on being promoted into management, in many cases before they are ready. Sometimes, people want to be promoted because of their egos. Sometimes, they expect to move into management because of a limited career track. Whatever the reason, we promote people every day who are not ready for management roles. In fact, many of us promote associates based on qualities and a track record that demonstrate that they will fail. Why? Because we promote people based on the jobs they are doing now, as opposed to the jobs into which they would be moving.

Within an organization we have a responsibility not only to new managers, but to all employees of the organization. When we promote individuals who are not ready, we not only play Russian roulette with their careers, but we are gambling with all of those with whom these individuals work. Once the damage is done it is difficult to repair. It is easy to understand the fallout from promoting those not ready when we look at the common traits of and mistakes made by new leaders.

Your bench strength as an organization, and your levels of employee engagement, relate directly to the strengths of your newer leadership. Most organizations promote people for being great problem solvers, not for being leaders. Many leaders fail or fall short in their first two to three years because of this. Some of the common traits of new managers, as well as some common frailties are described below.

Tunnel Vision

Most new leaders become leaders because they were good at something. They made names for themselves in a certain area of the organization and they produced results. When they are promoted to a managerial role, they tend to stay focused on those things with which they are comfortable. New managers may have a difficult time seeing how a group or department's choices and actions impact others. In some cases, these new managers may ignore certain data or people, even within their own departments, because of tunnel vision. Because these individuals have a difficult time seeing the connections between departments, or how their areas fit into the bigger picture, they have a difficult time with strategic thinking and planning. Many of the choices they make may be good for one area of the organization, but at the expense of others or the organization as a whole. They do not coordinate with key stakeholders and colleagues nor attempt to gain buy-in from others on change initiatives.

Know-All Syndrome

Another challenge new managers face is letting go of what they are "experts" at. Their knowledge base may be an inch wide and a mile deep; but they need to move toward a knowledge base that is a mile wide and an inch deep. This creates stress for new leaders. Many of them have their identity wrapped up in their expertise. Because of the need to feel in control, new managers tend to provide the answers, solve the problems, and try to do the work for the people who report to them. Many also feel that they can do a better job than others. Here is the rub: the managers' expertise causes them to try to do the work of others, which in turn creates a bottleneck because any one manager cannot produce as much work as several individuals. People stop trying, because they know the manager will intercede, redo their work, or even take over. Productivity drops, and organizational performance suffers.

We see this type of scenario very clearly with sales. I have had promote one of their best sales people. Within a short time, the sale pipeline has shrunk and so have sales. When they look for the reason, they find it is the manager's micro-management. Unfortunately, the sales manager believes he or she can sell and service customers better than employees can. Whether is it is true or not really does not matter, and the manager starts working on all of the proposals, asks sales representatives to schedule calls and meetings with customers around his or her schedule, and creates policies that force sales people to go to the manager for approval on even the most inane decisions. Unfortunately, one sales manager cannot produce what five sales associates can.

Communication Dexterity

The communication skills needed for leadership positions are more varied and advanced than those required for individuals. If you think about it, individual contributors spend most of their time working on assignments themselves, sometimes in teams, and in front of customers. They are rewarded and recognized for doing great work. The better they are at their work, the more likely a manager or an organization will put up with difficult behavior (an approach I am not advocating). We would prefer our employees to work through conflict, but we will in many cases settle for an employee who is deft enough not to start conflict. The most interesting aspect of an individual contributor is that their communication becomes somewhat predictable based on the scope and tasks of their roles.

On the other hand, leaders must respond to multiple stakeholders, have less predictability in their jobs, and find more ambiguity in their work. These factors create a need for strong communication skills. Leaders must work cross-functionally; work across boundaries; deal with the public; work with employees and executives; maintain confidences while attempting to remain authentic; have access to information that is controversial and confidential; motivate employees, creating an inclusive environment and promoting a stable outward appearance.

If you look at a hotel, for example, front-desk employees can be surprised at times, but they know the process they will use to check guests. They know the majority of questions they will receive throughout the day, and the majority of their time is focused on one stakeholder . . . the guest. We can and should expect more from our employees, but if we have a front-desk associate who is friendly, courteous, and competent with our guests, we will most likely be satisfied.

A general manager at a hotel has to consistently work with the guests, a management team, front-desk personnel, maintenance, food and beverage, housekeeping, sales, community organizations, brand personnel from a corporate entity, possibly a management company including a supervisor, and an ownership group. A general manager's day is filled with many surprises and requests from a variety of directions. These individuals must deal with problems, conflicts, performance issues, administrative responsibilities—and then not forget to catch people doing things well and celebrate success.

At the end of the day, a good leader must have a strong ability to communicate to different types of people, in different types of situations, without a great deal of notice or predictability. That requires a robust skill set to be successful, and one of the key ingredients is communication dexterity.

Self-Interest

It is impossible to be curious about others when we are concerned with ourselves. Being human means that we protect ourselves and those close to us. How does that play out on a daily basis? Our emotional reactions are faster than our rational thoughts. For example, if you were standing outside, your child ran out in the parking lot of a busy shopping center, and a car was coming at your child, you would not stop and think about the consequences, possible solutions, and the best course of action. No, you would run out and protect your child. If you were asked why you did what you did, you would most likely say it was a natural reaction. You might say something like, "I just did what I did. I did not even think about it."

Our work lives are very similar. We have many emotional responses that we then justify after the fact with rational thinking. As new managers, we have just left an environment that expects us to be driven, desirous of career movement, caring about what others think of our work, and craving recognition. That works well when we are in positions that reflect ourselves and our work. As managers, our work is about others and the broader business. This is a time to retrain ourselves and move from "me" to "we."

What stops us from making that shift is our self-interest. Many new managers take credit for their teams' work because of an emotional need for recognition. That need is self-centered. So is the need to move up or advance in one's career. Self-interest will always be there. I am not implying in any way that you should not care about what others think or that your career progression is not important, only that it is not the basis for managing people or functions and that we must temper our personal needs in order to be successful. Too many new managers take a stand, innovate, propose a process change, or whatever, based on how it will impact their careers rather than how it will impact their businesses.

Recently, I experienced this phenomenon with an internal consultant at a company. He wanted to add value in every consult he had with different groups in the company—a very admirable goal. However, the need to add value became so important that he spent his time thinking about how to do that while meeting with the internal customer. The irony is that his agenda for providing added value every time became a self-interested quest, causing him difficulty in doing the very thing he set out to do. He could not hear the important issues dropped right in front of him because he was no longer curious.

Our egos, agendas, or everyday distractions stop us from being curious about others. They stop us from being present in the moment and present a particular vulnerability for new managers because they rely too much on being experts and their own perspectives, rather than understanding their employees' perspectives and the knowledge their employees bring with them. Relationships are built on a foundation that requires two people. It is difficult to invest in someone who is overly invested in him- or herself. An individual who is too invested in him- or herself will not help others unless it helps them. They are not going to grow others, mentor or coach them, and if they do, others will question their motives. But the challenges do not stop there.

A Story About Fear

Since I have become sick my life has changed significantly. I have lost my hair and some weight, changed my diet, and I obviously do not feel as well as I used to. My schedule has changed because I can no longer keep up my old pace. But I am still going and I am still fighting. I will get through this. I truly appreciate all of the thoughts and prayers my friends have sent my way. It is that very sentiment that helps me keep going, keep fighting the fight. My family has been wonderful, and so have my co-workers. One of my colleagues even shaved his head to support me. He said he would not grow his hair back until I am able to grow mine. But not everyone has been that supportive.

I am noticing something I have never noticed before, probably because I never experienced it before I was sick. I first noticed the spectacle last week. People have been treating me differently. People do not look me in the eye. The other day, as I was grocery shopping, I smiled and said hello to a clerk. He looked away as if he did not see me, acted nervous as if he would catch something, and then walked away.

When I went to my child's school for the talent show, I could not help but notice some parents looking at me and quickly glancing away when I looked at them. Some of the parents even whispered to each other as they made quick glances my way, hoping I would not notice. I get it. I no longer fit the norm. I am different. I now have a label; I am ill. Luckily, I have a respite from it at times. I forget at times how I look, that I have lost all of my hair, until I look in the mirror.

I am reminded by small moments that I am still the same person I have always been and that the spectacle is more about the other people than about me. Shortly after the talent show, we went to dinner. Two people came up to our table. One of them asked me how my treatment was going and the other shared a story about his wife who survived and became cancer-free. Both of these individuals were truly concerned. I did not know either of them, and yet they made a connection with me in a split second.

I realized right then that there are two types of people. The first are those people who act out of compassion and opportunity, who smile and say hello to a person in a wheelchair. And then there are the types who are filled with apprehension or fear, the ones who look away and pretend you are not there. I can only say I treasure the moments when I meet the people who smile and provide well wishes. I know it makes me feel better.

Fear

The story above is actually a compilation of a number of stories I have heard from people I know who have fallen ill or who have a disability. They quickly realize that being different means that certain people become uncomfortable around them. This same behavior holds true in various aspects of our lives, especially organizational life.

- The new salesperson who complains about making cold calls because the rejections make her uncomfortable.
- The consultant who does not ask a question or make a certain recommendation because he is are afraid of what the client's response might be.
- The employee who does not provide feedback to her supervisor because she is afraid of repercussions.
- The manager who takes credit for the work of one of his employees because he is afraid of how he will be perceived if it is known that it was not his idea.

I like to ask clients to play devil's advocate. Typically, we only look at one side of the risk equation. If we take the above scenarios and turn them around, we can see what that other side looks like.

- What if I, a new salesperson, do not make cold calls? What are the consequences? How do those consequences compare with the consequences of rejection?
- What if I, as the consultant, do not ask an important question of a client? What if I do not make a certain recommendation because I am afraid of what the client's response might be? How does that impact the future relationship? How does that impact the value I bring to the relationship? What about the trust level between the client and myself?
- What if I do not provide feedback to my supervisor? How will the situation improve? How will it impact other employees? New employees? My manager's career?
- What if I take credit for my employee's work? How will that impact my relationship with my employee? What about the rest of the team? What will this do to the overall productivity

of the department? How will it impact my ability to attract internal candidates? Will people in my department want to transfer to another role and department?

Fear is a funny thing. Fear and risk are a two-sided coin, but we often only look at one side of that coin, and when we do, the results can be, at best, a hindrance because they hold us back. At worst, these types of actions can be absolutely devastating. Fear can paralyze us. Some say it can motivate, but my experience says differently. Fear causes us to take small actions when big ones are necessary or the perceived safe route, even when it is damaging. Progress needs to be measured against a success measure, not progress for progress' sake. If I sold $1,000,000 worth of product, is that success? Not if my actions actually stopped me from selling $3,000,000 worth of product and damaged a client relationship along the way because I took the safe route. From my experience, fear is about risk, and when there is risk people try to mitigate the risk. When we are focused to reduce risk, we are not focused on increasing opportunity.

New managers face risk.

- The risk of others making them look bad because they are no longer doing the work, yet they are accountable for the work f others;
- The new risk of compensation that they no longer control because much of it may be based on the productivity of others; and
- The risk of "What if they figure me out?"

Most of us have self-doubts at some point in our careers, usually during changes and transitions, whether into a new career, industry, or when we transition into a management position.

If we lack self-doubt, then we most likely have a huge ego, which would mean we are very narcissistic—self-interested. Assuming we are not too self-interested, we can say that we have doubts from time to time, which is normal. And assuming it is normal and we want to mitigate these self-doubts, what should new managers do? Well, if we choose to act on our fear we will try not to show the self-doubts, and we will most likely attempt to cover them up. Some individuals will choose to act with a great deal of bravado; others become defensive; and still others hide in an office until 5:00 p.m. Either way, new managers are still in a very difficult position. Generally speaking, new managers, as well as the rest of us, are not working in what we would consider safe, healthy environments. Unhealthy environments squash candor and the ability to be vulnerable, making it even more likely that a new leader will choose to act out of fear and risk rather than opportunity, causing a vicious cycle.

Many people in these types of situations quit or are fired. Those who last can go through a painful process, usually beginning with counseling from a superior or results of a 360-degree feedback tool that often feels like a slap in the face. Most of these new managers are surprised by the feedback they receive. If a manager is having trouble, even if he or she is aware of the trouble, much energy is spent in protection mode trying to look capable. Candid feedback can fly in the face of such efforts, causing individuals to become defensive and take their frustrations out on their teams or to run away, which in the professional world means to quit or avoid uncomfortable interactions. Either makes the situation worse.

Sometimes organizations deal with these issues well and can help new leaders do the only thing that will help the situation— work through the fear rather than act on it. The sad aspect of these types of situations is that these people were promoted for a reason. They were superstars! These individuals were on what many call the "fast track" because the company was so impressed with their ability to solve problems, be creative, and get work done. The person's star did not fade because of some Jekyll and Hyde syndrome. He did not all of a sudden lose his talent on the way to work. The person's star faded because he was not ready to lead.

Organizations need to promote and develop leaders in a way that strengthens new managers and allows them to be authentic. Most new managers are concerned because everything that made them successful in the past could cause them to fail in their new roles. The paradox is that they need the past experience and success to be credible as new managers. It is difficult to attain authenticity when you are filled with fear, act on ego, and now handle more data, tasks, and work, with more people creating more distractions than you have ever had to deal with before.

Succession Planning

In order to support new managers, an organization must be clear regarding managerial or leadership expectations. (See Table 9.3.) What does leadership look like at this level in this organization? It is imperative to have clear criteria published for everyone to see. Some employees desire moving into managerial positions because they have an idyllic view of what being a manager involves. They talk about how much easier it is to be a manager, and have a common perception of having more control, less stress, more pay, and others to do all of the work for you. If these employees only knew the truth, they might not desire a promotion. An organization can begin to shift this view of management by sharing what is expected.

Once clear criteria are developed and published, an organization can focus on succession planning and treat it as an inclusive process. The reasons for this are

- *The fluid nature of employment these days.* People leave organizations only to return a few years later. If you want employees to come back, you will want them to know that you believe in investing in them.
- *Retention of your employees.* Employees stick around for a variety of reasons. They stay in organizations that help

Table 9.3 Example of Competencies for a New Leader

Competency	Summary
Communication	Creates an atmosphere for open communication
Client Focus	Effectively understands client needs and expectations
Networking	Builds networks, alliances, and team spirit
Planning	Successfully translates strategy into action
Building and Developing Talent	Invests appropriate time and resources into developing and hiring the right people
Performance Leadership	Acts with integrity and creates an inclusive environment
Conflict Management	Works through challenging situations with people in a win-win manner
Managing Change	Promotes change in a productive and positive approach
Leadership	Helps others understand the big picture and align with the organization's direction

Source: Realtime Performance

them grow. Employees want their skills to remain sharp. In fact, only 12 percent of employees leave for more money.[3]

- *Difficulty finding people with the right skill sets.* If we exclude employees from growth opportunities, then we make it difficult to fill internal positions because we lack enough people with the appropriate skill sets.

- *You never know.* We tend to exclude certain employees because they are not the current star, and we include others because they are current stars. However, as we have just demonstrated, current status does not determine future performance.

We recommend that organizations look at succession planning as a "roundabout," a kind of street intersection at which traffic comes into a one-way flow around a middle isle. Some characteristics of a roundabout are

- Incoming motor vehicles give way to motor vehicles already in the roundabout. That means that motor vehicles already in the roundabout have the right of way.
- Lower speeds are used to prevent accidents.
- Different traffic lanes lead to different places and at different speeds.
- Parking is not an option in the roundabout.
- Pedestrians may not loiter around or on the middle isle.
- While all motor vehicles move around the middle isle in the same direction, they can get on or off in multiple places.[4]

As shown in Figure 9.1, the analogy can fit an organization. First, the middle isle or center is the organization. All traffic or development revolves around the organization and the organization's needs. Sometimes in the era of inclusion we have forgotten this basic tenet. Second, all of the traffic is moving in the same direction, which essentially means that everyone is working, growing, developing, and moving in the same direction, while at the same time each individual has a different path and a different set of needs. But if we are all focused on the vision and mission of an organization, most everything we do should enhance that effort. As employees, we are expected not to hang out or to coast. Each employee might be moving at a different speed or focus on a different path, but we should all be growing and available for opportunities. Some employees will choose to get off the round-about and take a road to another organization. If this is handled well, there won't be an accident as the employee exits. Employees should have the opportunity to come back at a later time when there is a better match between their needs and the organization's.

As an organization, we have a responsibility to create an environment with the same types of characteristics as a roundabout,

Figure 9.1 Roundabout Succession Model

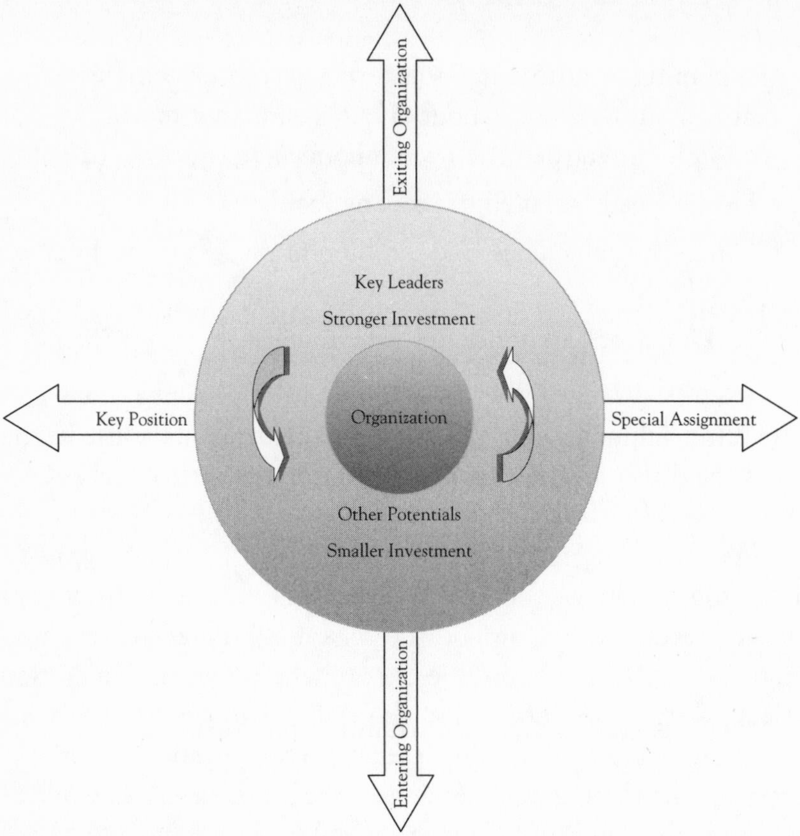

Source: Performancepoint, LLC

which means we must find a way to invest in everyone appropriately while keeping our focus on the organization as a whole. This is a significantly different approach from the way succession planning is often approached. Most organizations are used to separating and labeling employees and then investing in small groups.

Earlier, I said current status does not determine future performance. However, the best predictor of future success is past success. If someone has successfully achieved something before, then he or she will most likely be able to achieve it again.

The odds are increased when the person has been able to accomplish tasks multiple times in various situations and settings and has achieved results. Now, it may seem contradictory to apply this to the transition to leadership, but if the best predictor of future performance is past performance, then we know that an employee will be successful in his or her current role if he or she has already been successful in a similar role or at similar work activities. So the best way to see whether someone has the capability to be a leader is to provide opportunities to learn about leadership and practice leadership skills while still in an individual contributor role.

Many organizations train employees on leadership skills prior to their being promoted into supervisory roles. Training like this should include what leadership means and how employees will need to adapt if they attempt to move into a managerial role. Some of the approaches an organization should utilize include:

- Assessments and feedback related to competencies needed for leadership;
- Leadership development training that focuses on the emotional and mindset shifts needed to be successful when transitioning;
- Job assignments that allow leadership skills to be observed prior to any job change;
- Case studies to allow employees to think more broadly and start building a network to be effective; and
- Realistic job previews to help employees decide whether they want to move into a supervisory role.

After employees are exposed to leadership responsibilities and have assessed their strengths and potential liabilities when it comes to taking a leadership position, they should then participate in a selection process. The first aspect of such a process should be a realistic job preview that helps employees determine whether they are ready for supervisory roles. This is an effective way to reduce the number of internal candidates for a managerial position. Each candidate should, at minimum, be interviewed and tested to determine whether he or she is ready for a managerial role.

The actual transition can still be a challenge for many individuals, so it is important that an organization have a transition plan. New managers should have leadership development plans that clearly lay out at least their first ninety days. New leaders should receive feedback from their peers, employees, and supervisor at the end of that time.

As people move into managerial roles, they may feel alone. It becomes inappropriate for them to talk with other employees about certain things, and in many cases it is difficult to talk with one's own supervisor. A new leader needs a mentor and/or a coach. You can help new leaders transition by providing peer groups, coaching programs, new leader mentoring programs, or using a mentoring or coaching service. The most important thing is creating a safe environment that allows new leaders to be vulnerable, and thus to learn.

The Leadership Readiness Matrix (Figure 9.2) is a tool that will assist you in determining whether your employees are ready

Figure 9.2 Leadership Readiness Matrix

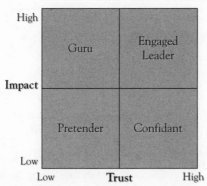

Source: Performancepoint, LLC

to lead. It can also be an excellent coaching tool to utilize with anyone who may be interested in transitioning.

The Leadership Readiness Matrix looks at two axes—trust and impact. These two axes have a direct correlation to self-interest and fear. The more self-interested you are, the less trust you will have in your relationships. The more you let fear influence your decisions and actions, the less impact you will have. Your ability to develop trusted relationships with impact will land you in one of four categories, described below.

Confidant. A *confidant* is a person who can be trusted with information, but will not challenge another's thinking. This person is like a vault. You can tell them anything or vent to this person. But he or she will not necessarily help you achieve more or succeed. They provide half of the equation when it comes to leadership.

Pretender. *Pretenders* act as if they are ready to lead. They are often not self-aware or concerned with their own deficiencies. People at this point in their development look at events and analyze them based on how they are impacted. Not only are such people self-interested, but they also focus on minimizing risk.

Guru. *Gurus* are experts. These are smart people who know their stuff. We need these people for advice, solutions, innovative ideas, and their basic technical expertise. However, we will probably get a second opinion. We know that a guru sometimes has agendas, distractions, and an ego. Their advice can be colored at times, and they do not always make us smarter. Sometimes they just want us to accept their perspectives.

Engager. An *engager* is ready to lead. This is an individual who is able to temper his or her self-interest. Engagers are curious about others and their needs. Engagers do not worry about how decisions will impact them. They focus on growing other people and helping others succeed. Engagers are motivated by creating opportunities for colleagues and work in an open manner. They are more than willing to challenge us, but in a professional way.

Questions to Ask Yourself

- What is our current process for promotions?
- How do we help ensure the success of our new leaders?
- What is our success rate with new leaders?
- How do we hinder the success of our new leaders?
- To what extent is our environment safe for new leaders?
- How should our succession process change to better support a strong new leadership pipeline?

10

WHAT IS YOUR MPV?

In This Chapter

▶ Engaged Versus Victim Mentality

▶ Personal Engagement Connections

▶ Personal Engagement Competencies

▶ Personal Engagement Matrix

It used to be commonly accepted that people joined companies and left managers. Now, more and more professionals are leaving organizations in order to move their careers forward. They desire new challenges, special job assignments, and a sense that they are staying sharp and learning. Until recently, many organizations have taken a great deal of responsibility for developing their employees. But it has become clear that employees should be taking more accountability for their own growth, their careers, and their engagement. They should ask: "What is my professional value (MPV)"? Employees should manage their MPV carefully.

When you ask employees to think about a time when they were engaged in their work or their organization and to describe what that time was like, you will most likely get back a positive set of answers. You will be able to see the excitement in the room as they remember and share their thoughts. Some of the responses I have heard in our sessions with clients include:

- Challenged
- Learned new things
- Felt trusted by others, including my managers
- Felt safe to take risks
- Had lots of energy
- Believed in what I was doing
- More productive

When we ask employees whether they would like to feel engaged more frequently and for longer periods of time, we hear a resounding "Yes!" Employees want to succeed in something they believe in. They want to have fun succeeding. And they want to trust the people and organization they work with while doing so. While that may be true, very few get their wishes. Employees have a difficult time staying engaged for a number of reasons. Until recently, the number one reason referenced was "my manager." We are concerned by this too quick and too simple view of employee engagement. Let's see why the manager has been seen as the core of employee engagement and explore that a bit further.

Managers are employees of an organization, as well. We have already acknowledged some of the challenges that leaders face, whether newly transitioned or experienced, but what of their other challenges? Managers also struggle to keep themselves engaged and connected to the organization. Managers face change just like employees do and have the added challenge of pushing people in a direction they may not agree with. Sandwiched in the middle, managers have an especially difficult time thinking about their own development and careers, because they must focus on others, and as they move up in an organization they will receive less feedback and recognition, and incur more risk.

Organizations that have embraced the manager as the employee engagement solution have put manager compensation, and sometimes promotions, at risk based on the results of engagement efforts. That is a lot of weight on the back of managers. We have seen that those backs start to break in two to five years and, after initial success, the progress and organization that have been established begin to wane—hardly a scalable solution. As we noted earlier, several factors need to be monitored and managed to keep the organization functioning in employee engagement. Many of the drivers were identified earlier. But we have not explained why a reliance on the manager can be so damaging over time.

Engaged Versus Victim Mentality

When initial gains in employee engagement are not continued, by the time an organization recognizes what has happened, it is too late—the hole has been dug. It will take a long time for an organization to recover. Why? By focusing on only one aspect of the engagement equation (the manager), an organization discounts any others and promotes the idea that those other drivers have little or no value, power, or impact. The outcome is a culture with little or no accountability and personal responsibility for improving current conditions. In essence, those organizations have encouraged employees to become victims. Why should employees worry about how engaged they are and how to fix something when it is the managers' problem?

In order to create a culture in which employee engagement is embraced and is a shared responsibility, every employee must be educated about employee engagement and his or her role. Each employee needs to know how much impact he or she can have on the success of the organization, the team, and co-workers. Employees need to move along the continuum from powerless to powerful—becoming engaged versus being a victim. Characteristics of engaged individuals versus victims are shown in the following chart.

Engaged	Victim or Disengaged
Confidence	Apprehension
Opportunity	Risk
Growth	Stagnation
Innovation	Status quo
Committed	Indifferent
Authentic	Fake
Ownership	Blame
Creative and resourceful	Unimaginative

We can see the difference between a person who is engaged and one who is not. The distinction is even easier to see in a crisis. Remember this scenario?

The captain in a calm voice radioed air traffic control, "We're going to be in the Hudson."

"Emergency inbound," an air traffic controller states. He attempts to organize a way for a plane without any engines to land at Teterboro airport located in New Jersey.

"Can I get him in for Runway One?" the LaGuardia controller asks the Teterboro tower.

"Runway One, that's good," the Teterboro tower controller responds.

"1529 turn right two-eight-zero," the LaGuardia tower tells the pilot to get the plane to Teterboro.

"We can't do it," the pilot says.

"Which runway would you like at Teterboro?" asks LaGuardia.

"We're going to be in the Hudson," the pilot says.

Well, we all know what happened next. Captain Chesley "Sully" Sullenberger landed the plane safely in the river and

Figure 10.1 Personal Engagement Model

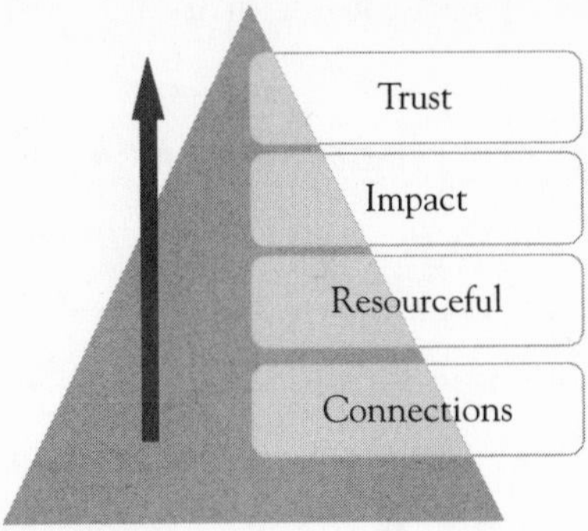

Source: Performancepoint, LLC

everyone on that plane survived. While he used words like "sickening" and "disbelief" to explain his initial reactions, he overcame those feelings quickly. He never waited for manager or union approval or said, "Please help me or we will die." He took responsibility. He made a conscious choice to manage his emotions; quickly reviewed his training; picked a course of action; and remained calm. This hero chose to spend his few moments working through what he could impact.[1]

Knowing the difference between being engaged and being a victim is one thing. How to create a path toward being engaged is another. One model we suggest using is the Personal Engagement Model seen in Figure 10.1.

Personal Engagement Connections

The first thing that employees need to understand is that the number and strength of their connections to their work and to the organization will determine how engaged they are. The second thing they should recognize is that they have significant influence, and in some cases control, of many of those connections. They are not victims. Here are just some of the links they can influence:

- Career plans;
- Development and growth;

- Co-worker relationships;
- Team relationships and functioning;
- Networking;
- Cross-departmental relationships and teamwork;
- Connecting their work to the organization's strategy;
- Manager relationships;
- Local work environment;
- Connecting personal values to the organizational culture;
- Building relationships with senior leadership;
- Understanding senior leadership decisions and direction; and
- Managing personal and professional transitions.

Connections are important because they create some important outcomes. The first outcome is that employees stay longer because they have many reasons to stay. The second outcome is that employees are much more productive as a direct result of the connections they have made. The more connections an employee has made, the more resourceful he or she becomes. Having a number of connections to the organization helps us as employees to be less self-interested. We begin to buy into something larger than ourselves. The more resourceful we become, the more impact we have. Connected employees seem to be able to take a project, customer relationship, or idea to a higher level. They don't just complete tasks and check them off. They work with a sense of meaning. The more impact we have, the more trust people have in us, and the more trust we have in others and in ourselves.

The mutually beneficial bonds make a significant difference. The more we are connected to our work and organization, the longer we stay and the more productive we will be. Part of this phenomenon comes from the connections themselves, but the rest comes from the art of building and growing our connections. We have to temper our own self-interest to build connections, creating more trust in the process. Our comfort allows us to produce more, come up with creative ideas, and focus on important issues instead of being distracted by what others may think, unhelpful gossip, or potential risks.

Personal Engagement Competencies

Building and growing connections is an entirely different story under difficult circumstances when we are most challenged and our true colors are displayed. In order for employees to stay centered, they must master certain competencies. Some samples of personal engagement competencies pertinent to managers and others are seen in Exhibit 10.1.

Exhibit 10.1 Personal Engagement Competencies

1. *Personal Responsibility:* I take responsibility for my actions and their outcomes. I am willing to state my needs and ideas clearly and constructively. I take charge of my career and the connections I can make and influence at work. I consistently act with honesty and authenticity, demonstrating respect for myself and others. I work in accordance with my values. I am aware of my needs, preferences, strengths, and challenges.

2. *Inclusion:* I recognize the unique contributions that each individual makes. I reduce barriers to success for everyone. I am aware of how my actions and reactions can impact others. I am able to interact with people who are different from me.

3. *Change-Resilience:* I am flexible and willing to change. I can be a role model in promoting productive change. I consistently demonstrate adaptability. I am willing to help others see how to change and how that change will affect them personally.

4. *Growing Self and Others:* I take responsibility for my own learning and career. I graciously accept feedback from others

on a regular basis. I invest appropriate time and resources in developing myself. I have sought out a coach or mentor to increase own contribution and marketability. I provide feedback to others on a regular basis; I invest my time in helping others succeed and grow.

5. Service-Centered: I take time to understand my customers' (internal or external) needs. I make an every effort to surpass expectations. I plan my work based on the impact it will have on others especially my customers. I develop and maintain powerful relationships with my customers.

Source: Performancepoint, LLC

Personal Responsibility

The very first competency than needs to be tackled is *personal responsibility*. We must teach employees that they have the ability to change their corners of the world and a responsibility to themselves and to others to do so. In our workshops, it is clear that the terms "accountability" and "ownership" have been watered down. Employees in many organizations feel powerless, have observed less than stellar behavior, or are afraid to be really accountable. We have seen that standards of accountability are much lower than needed in most organizations. Many people may admit responsibility, but don't take responsibility for the outcomes of their actions.

We see this type of behavior in all walks of life. Even our country's leadership has lowered standards. One example is when Vice President Dick Cheney cursed at Senator Patrick Leahy and then said he had no regrets.[2] He admitted his actions, but took very little responsibility for them or their outcomes. In fact, his behavior had an impact on what young people view as acceptable behavior and, more importantly, influenced the FCC's ability to punish broadcasters regarding the use of these same curse words.[3] We must move closer to a culture of 100 percent accountability. We must raise our standards if we are to excel. Accountability ensures transparency and sheds light on even the darkest recesses of our organizations.

Over a period of time working in a stressful environment, at a fast pace, with more work than hours, we must make choices based on our preferences at that moment. Usually the more difficult choices mean making sacrifices. When we decide to sacrifice one thing for another, we are reflecting our values. For instance, an individual may value achievement and may value family. Over time, the person will make choices regarding work such as traveling, overtime, and special assignments that impact the family. In some cases, those choices may cause that person to say no to coaching his son's Little League team, not attend games, limit family time, and say yes to a commuting assignment so that he is only home on weekends, and so forth.

In the moment, the decisions made may not seem that difficult or may even be fairly easy to make, but over time the scale goes out of balance, and this person will have a problem. The natural response when this occurs is for the person to react emotionally. For instance, if this person's family is frustrated, maybe to the degree that his wife wants a divorce, he will journey in one of two directions—react negatively to his family because of the pressure from them, or react negatively to his organization because of the impact it has had on his family. You might hear this individual say things like, "Don't you get it? I have made these sacrifices for you!" or "I have given up everything for this company and what have I gotten back—nothing except possibly a divorce." Either way, he has now become a victim who is no longer taking responsibility for his choices.

To take personal responsibility, a person must be self-aware, understand his or her needs, preferences, values, and talents. Employees need to find ways to connect their personal attributes to their work and work life; to work in accordance with who they are currently, all the while striving to improve themselves. For this very reason, development needs to be a process and dialogue a constant. We may lose our edge over time and it is likely that we will not recognize it while it is happening. Every time my firm works with clients on values clarification, we find that employees are challenged by the exercise. Most of us do not know what our values really are, and even if we do, we probably have not narrowed them down and prioritized them. Even if we have worked on our values, it most likely has five years or more since then, and to what extent have we lived up to them?

Inclusion

Our ability to have empathy for others and accept the value that others bring is of key importance to engagement. This is because we as individuals have a significant ability to either over-blow or downplay the engagement of others. Our ability to recognize the value that others bring, to appreciate how they differ from us, and to understand how we impact them inherently reflects our ability to include others. It means we have an interest in others and are paying attention to them and their needs. The only way we are able to include others is to temper our own self-interest and our need to be right.

Individuals and organizations sometimes view inclusion in extreme terms. Some people believe inclusion is a bunch of hooey. They believe their way is the right way and that other ways are not as solid. They feel that others should *earn* their trust. They are less flexible than their colleagues and want others to change their ways to meet their own particular needs. Those at the other extreme view inclusion as of the utmost importance. They believe everyone brings something special to a project and has high potential. They want to throw out labels altogether and are willing to ignore accountability to help everyone fit in. They believe that every answer has value and neglect to distinguish whether it will work or not. The one extreme is too exclusionary and the other too inclusive. We need a middle ground. Everyone deserves a fair chance to participate and add value. Each person should be recognized for what he or she brings to the table. Everyone should feel like part of the team. Each person should be developed and expected to perform at the highest level possible. But in the end, there are individual differences and they cannot be ignored, although they should not be highlighted in inappropriate or unhelpful ways.

Change-Resilience

Change-resilience is a fundamental skill not usually taught in organizations. In fact, most training on change is process-oriented and focuses on how to implement change, while the majority of the time our challenges come from those individuals who are change-resistant. It is sometimes difficult to predict who will be resistant and who will not be resistant, because change is a personal issue. Mainly, we function in a self-protective way, so when under stress we may let our emotions rule.

An example is when an organization puts into place a standard for referrals in the sales process. Your best salesperson could be the biggest challenge in terms of meeting the new standard. Why? He or she has been great—a real blessing when it comes to meeting the numbers. Why would the person resist change? Obviously, a salesperson who is successful has less incentive to change. Second, reaction to change is very personal. That salesperson could harbor guilt about asking someone for a referral. This could stem from a time when someone asked for something and he or she felt uncomfortable. The situation may not even have had anything to do with referrals directly. The salesperson just has an emotional trigger that leads to resistance of the new method. And the salesperson will generally spend time trying to resist the change rather than asking the benefits of the change.

Employees need the skill set to be able to see benefits in a change, to employ personal change strategies, to measure their own progress, and find ways to celebrate their own success during change efforts. Now, this should not absolve the organization or the manager from the responsibility of leading a change effort well. But employees can "write their own story," utilize a shared language with the organization regarding change and make it personal to them.

Growing Self and Others

Over the past several years, we seem to have had less time and more work. It is difficult to keep up. We also know that span of control for management has increased over the years. I have one client currently who is increasing the minimum number of people who report to any one manager as an efficiency effort. Unfortunately, that means that those managers have less time and energy to help shepherd direct reports' careers. Thus, it is especially important for employees to learn how to grow themselves and take responsibility for their own success and career development.

Your career is one of the most important investments you can make. When we invest in our retirement, we do not just drop the money off to an individual or company and then forget about it. We follow our dollars and we pay attention to whether our investments are paying off or not. We research, read about, or talk through our investment choices to make sure we are comfortable. In many cases, we identify the type of investor weare, based on our tolerance for risk. The more comfortable we are with our investments and our financial advisors, the more likely we are to keep our money not only in those investments, but also with that advisor.

What makes us comfortable with an advisor and our investments? Trust and involvement. We need to trust the advisor and the information being shared with us, and we need to take a strong role in our own investment strategy. In fact, our involvement, our ability to ask questions and make decisions, creates additional trust. The advisor who embraces our desire to play a role in our investment strategy is usually the most successful.

Careers are no different. Employees feel more comfortable when they take an active role in their career development.

Service-Centered

We like to work with others who have impact and make us think; make us smarter. We want our teammates to be resourceful and creative, with the ability to solve problems and to encourage us to do so. We prefer to work with people who are perceptive and catch the subtle cues around them. And we want to work with people who focus all of these talents and their energy on what creates success . . . the customer. It does not matter whether the customer is another department in the company or an actual person purchasing a product or a service. What matters is being service-minded—service-centered. When we are service-centered our egos are smaller, we concentrate on others, and our attention is centered on opportunities for success and how to solve problems, rather than on rules and bureaucracy.

How many of us have called the customer service department of a telephone company or cable company to work on a problem, only to be more frustrated when we hang up the phone? How many of us have had that similar experience multiple times with the same company? I know that I have. What that tells me is these customer service representatives are meeting company standards such as using the person's name at least five times in a conversation, even when it feels inauthentic, forced, or unnatural. Or they make sure to use the phrase, "Is there anything else I can help you with today?" before ending the call, even when they did not help you with your immediate problem. These customer service representatives and technical support personnel are following scripts, standards, and procedures. They are not focused on solving problems, showing empathy, or listening for our subtle or not so subtle cues. The result is disappointment. I would not want to work with the people at such an organization, let alone do business with them.

Personal Engagement Matrix

If you use feedback tools and training to teach employees personal engagement skills, you will promote more productivity and tenure. In my organization, we often use a personal engagement assessment with clients. This assessment enables them to measure and manage their progress with regard to specific connection actions emphasizing accountability, strategic focus, relationship building, innovation, and customer focus. It is most important that each employee sees the opportunity to achieve more and to help others achieve more. It is not about leadership or higher goals; it is about how we work and interact with others, our work, and the organization as a whole. (See Figure 10.2.)

A person can play one of four key roles in an organization. When I refer to roles, I am not talking about positions or career development. These roles are reflective of engagement and healthy versus non-healthy behaviors. Of the four roles, two are positive; of the two positive roles, one is a much stronger, more helpful role.

Victim

The first role is that of a highly disengaged individual who has probably made choices that have compromised his or her values. An individual in this category personalizes most things and in a negative manner. Such people are passive aggressive and under certain circumstances can become outwardly negative. They are considered *victims* because they focus on themselves and usually act on the basis of limiting risk and avoidance. Victims use confidential mechanisms to complain because it feels safer, and will most likely not share potential solutions. All they can see is the problem. We tend to lack trust in these individuals and do not see them as having impact—at least not positive impact.

Figure 10.2 Personal Engagement Matrix

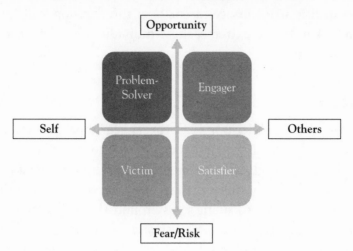

Satisfier

A similar role is the *satisfier*. These individuals also act out of fear and concern, but are not outwardly negative. Satisfiers may be frightened or concerned, but will try to put on a positive face. They want to help move in the right direction, but will provide safe answers or answers they believe others will receive positively. Unfortunately, even with all good intentions, they will have little impact because they are not thinking about the customer or the organization, and they are not thinking about achievement and opportunity. We trust these individuals, but most likely do not view them as having impact.

Problem-Solver

The next engagement role is the *problem-solver*. Problem-solvers work hard and help to move the organization forward. They look for opportunities and are less concerned with risk. These individuals are focused, reliable, and maintain a solid level of engagement. But these people are challenged in that they lack a broader view of the organization. Individual contributors see the organization through their lenses and will have a tendency to tie decisions to an agenda or how the decision will impact them. Taken to the extreme, these individuals can be viewed as opportunistic.

Engager

The last role is the *engager*. Engagers see opportunities when others see pitfalls and help everyone around them solve problems. Engagers are trusted because they are curious about others and can temporarily suspend their own agendas. These individuals are perceptive to subtle cues around them, and they hold themselves to high accountability standards. They are present in the moment and spend more time trying to understand others, versus making others understand them. They are able to influence people while staying open to being influenced. These are the people we trust who also have impact.

As stated earlier, MPV means "managing your Professional value" or "my professional value." Each employee has one. As inclusive as we want to be, some employees will have more value to an organization or even to an industry than others. Each employee needs to understand what components make up his or her professional value and how to manage them. This is about employees taking ownership and accountability for what they contribute to an organization, and making sure to take control of their careers. It is important to corporations as well as individuals. It is not just about "fit" when you hire someone; it is about maintaining that fit and helping the employee grow with you. This is a mind shift for employees and for organizations. However, it is a big opportunity for organizations. Helping employees understand their power and ability to create mutually beneficial bonds is a scalable effort that:

- Creates an ownership culture;
- Increases tenure; and
- Boosts productivity.

Imagine an organization in which every employee acts 100 percent accountable. Each employee acts like an owner in the way he or she thinks and make decisions. How far are we from that place? What if we could push the line out just a bit farther? Imagine the impact on your organization! Now imagine the impact on your people!

Questions to Ask Yourself

- How balanced are we in our approach to employee engagement?
- How scalable are our engagement efforts?
- To what extent are we placing an inappropriate amount of responsibility on our managers?
- What kind of culture are we building with our engagement efforts?
- How do we help employees understand how to connect to their work and organization?
- Beyond career development, how do support individuals drive their own engagement?
- To what extent do we have personal engagement skills at our organization?
- How do we currently develop personal engagement skills at our organization?
- How do we view accountability? How have we developed personal ownership?
- What percentage of our employees are victims? Satisfiers? Problem-solvers? Engagers?

11

EYE OF THE CUSTOMER

Everything we do as an organization should be focused on the customer. Unfortunately, politics, ego, fear, and self-interest often get in the way. Are we viewed as solely vendors? Are we reactive in serving our customers, or do we offer real value? Organizations that are actually customer focused, and show it through integrity-based actions and decisions, gain more loyalty from their customers because of a unique customer experience. These organizations are viewed as partners and their people as advisors, collaborators, and special. That experience is based on a culture that breeds employee engagement and customer focus.

Engagement and the Customer

Everything in this book reinforces the idea that relationships rule, collaboration is value, and that our systems and processes need to support that philosophy. In this fast-paced world with increased competition, we are all replaceable—both as individuals and as companies. The only way we ensure a long-lasting career or a sustainable organization is if we are able to stay competitive while building and maintaining relationships. So all of us have an incentive to redefine loyalty between the individual and the company, and the company and the individual. Rather than defining it solely on time with an organization, as in the past, why not define it on the quality of the relationship as well? We can elongate time with a company, but we will not reintroduce lifetime employment—at least not around the corner.

The type of economy in which we work has changed, and so has the worker. Employees are more knowledgeable, better educated, and have had the experience of seeing what happens to loyalists; they are let down by organizations just like everyone else. It is about success and keeping an organization alive. It's business. Organizations used to have productive command-and-control structures and a hierarchy, and these structures worked with lifetime employees who desired security. Employees knew that if they were good corporate citizens and followed directions well, they would have jobs. Because that arrangement no longer exists, employees want more. Today's workers want some say-so in decision making, change efforts, project planning, and other aspects of their work and work environments. Employees want to be treated as adults first before having to prove themselves. And employees demand to understand where the company is going and what is on the minds of senior leadership.

Gone are the days of "just put your time in and be patient." And a manager can no longer demand that an employee "shut up and do your job." In fact, a manager cannot think that way, because that attitude will show through to employees, even if the words are not explicitly stated. The reality is, we can no longer afford to just order employees around. We need to motivate, encourage, trust, advocate for, delegate to, grow, listen to, collaborate with, and take an interest in our employees. We need to lead. Too many managers today still think employees should feel lucky they have jobs, or at least a job in this particular organization. Many managers still walk into work with the attitude that they have people who work for them, rather than thinking about how they can support their employees. Ironically, this mentality does not start with a manager. It usually comes from the way an organization hires and on-boards, trains and develops employees and leaders, develops policies and procedures, and maintains a structure.

Service orientation in a hotel chain represents the influence of the management company, ownership, and brand perspectives. Sales practices at an organization are reflective of that particular organization's sales beliefs, compensation decisions, sales success measurements, accountability standards, and more. Companies that are distributed either hold a similar culture from location to location or operate differently based on structure, training, strength of a common vision, and so forth. We as organizations either invest in these efforts or we do not. Investment means more than "we held a training meeting." Investment means that, as an organization, we have made choices, sometimes difficult, to align our different efforts to promote a customer-based culture. Most importantly, employees are more engaged in cultures that are customer-centric. Employees want to do right by the customer, and when encouraged and supported, employees will do amazing things. Most recently Cornell University published a study making the case that a service-based environment was more important than employee satisfaction.[1] Our customers can tell the difference!

There are three core ways that an organization can ensure that they are customer-centric and support their employees' ability to focus on customers:

> *Sales:* The way we treat potential customers before they do business with us and the way we treat customers and potential customers during the buying process. Is the sales process about them or about us?

Service: The way we take care of our customers on a day-to-day basis. Is it rote service or are we curious about them? How well do we know our customers?

Consistent culture: How consistently does the culture behave when it comes to customers? Is the treatment different between service and sales? What about research and development or product fulfillment? How about in a distributed work environment?

Sales

A number of sales models view the customer as something to put up with. It is a rather old view of sales and is no longer very effective, unless you are the only game in town or you sell based on low price. Other models at least attempt to be consultative. Consultative models focus on asking questions that are relevant to the customer, but the questions typically start with and end with the vendor in mind. We subscribe to a more collaborative process that is truly customer-centric. No one knows the customer's business like he does, and rarely do people in an organization feel that they have someone with whom they can talk. If sales people are interested in their customers and can put down their "sales person" agenda for a short time, they will learn more. Why don't more companies and sales people take on more collaborative roles?

Product focus is very important to many organizations, especially small companies. Many smaller firms lack capital and work on a shoestring budget, causing an increased significance on growth and/or predictability. Growth and predictability are significant for all companies, but for small firms it can mean life or death. According to the Small Business Administration, only 40 percent of start-up businesses survive past six years.[2] To ensure success, many small business owners promote product pushing. This is the art of encouraging others to buy your product, even if it does not address their current problem.

Numerous organizations will actually try to find ways to either connect their product to the problem indirectly or redirect the client entirely, attempting to convince clients that they actually have a different problem. These efforts do not build trust, and in the few situations in which sale results, it is not worth the large numbers of customers who are turned off by the deception, inflexibility, pressure, and insincerity that accompany such tactics. Another result of this type of activity is the loss of good sales professionals who do not want to engage with customers in this way. I have also seen sales professionals sabotage a sale in order to protect their customers from these types of tactics.

It is significant to note that organizations that practice these tactics are not building strong relationships with their customers. When a customer feels strongly about a relationship with a sales person, the customer will keep up with the sales professional when he or she switches jobs, provide referrals, and explore multiple needs with the sales professional, even if the customer is not sure that the sales person has capability in that area. Customers will do this because they trust the sales professional and believe the person will help them think through their challenges. The by-product of these relationships is more opportunity and buy-in. The customer does not feel "sold" because he has had a problem-solving partner. By the time the sales person has attached any product or service to solving any problem, the customer has already helped to identify it.

We recently worked with an organization that was in the business of commodity sales. Product pushing was the sales strategy. Sales representatives had a catalog of products they could pull from. From a customer's perspective, it could be a draining experience working with one of these sales people. First, their customers were very busy and in many cases saw these calls as a distraction. Second, the sales calls could feel like a line-by-line review of catalog items. The sales representatives made choices about what items they would sell based on their commission potential or comfort with the product, rather than understanding their customers' needs. Note that this approach was indicative of one segment of the industry. However, other players n the industry began to change their approaches, and the new competitive environment impacted this business. Sales, profitability, and customer retention were all flattening or declining.

This organization carried on with the strengths and opportunities it did have, including:

- **Service:** Everyone was interested in creating positive relationships. The representatives enjoyed friendly interactions. When their existing customers experienced that service orientation, they appreciated it.
- **Value opportunity:** While it was clear that price made a difference in the industry, there were ways to create additional value for their customers.
- **People:** Employees were talented, determined, creative, and had resolve. They wanted to succeed, but they needed new approaches, techniques, and tools.
- **Market position:** While there was an increased amount of competition, this organization had an excellent track record for success, and there were still significant opportunities in the marketplace.

The challenges this organization faced in the sales group included:

- **Clarity of goals:** Individuals were unsure of the company and individual goals. Employees operated somewhat independently because they did not have common goals to pull them together.
- **Sales strategy:** There was a perception that sales strategy or best practices did not exist. There was agreement that lead generation and the expectations around the lead

assignments needed to be more clearly defined or tied to organizational strategy.

- **Accountability:** It was clear that a large percentage of people were not proactively selling. Lead generation activities were not being followed up, measured, or shared across the group.
- **Sales management:** People did not feel supported or coached along the way. They desired training, tools, and ongoing coaching. The current format for sales meetings lacked value. Communication must be clearer, more consistent, and celebratory.
- **Morale:** It was clear that morale was very low. The employees were under a great deal of stress. Between price erosion, competitor tactics, significant amounts of change in the industry, the perception of it being more difficult to make money, and the gap between sales people and management, they were finding it difficult to succeed.

A number of issues should have been looked at by this organization, but the first priority was, "How can we change the performance, in the short term, of this sales group in order to fund other improvements over time?"

The organization wanted to provide training to their sales professionals. Some of the challenges identified in the sales process included:

- Prospecting;
- Negotiation;
- Handling objections;
- Qualifying and connecting with prospects;
- Discovering and learning customer needs; and
- Growing the account and up-selling over time.

This represented a great deal of change for the sales representatives. Many did not react well to the changes. They had seen a lot of change already. There were people who actually spent time wishing for the good old days, almost expecting them to return. These sales people were going to have to change the way they worked individually, worked with customers, and with each other. Change itself can be frightening, but these sales people would have to use techniques that made them feel as if they were releasing control of the process, provided less opportunity for selling based on price, required that they work with fewer customers while increasing the profitability of the customers with whom they worked, emphasized increased customer retention, and required engaging in lead generation activities that would cause them to be rejected from time to time. Knowing that these sales people would need to break current habits and get out of their comfort zones, we knew training alone would not create the overall performance change the company was seeking.

This company needed to significantly increase the amount of new customer relationships in order to let go of some customer relationships that were no longer as profitable. Once that goal was in the process of being attained, the organization desired their sales people to sell at much higher value that they were; hoping to attain a 15 to 20 percent increase in profitability. However, to keep this up would be impossible unless this organization could fundamentally boost customer retention by at least 15 percent.

To accomplish their organizational sales goals, we first identified key ways in which the sales people could most effectively improve their performance. We had three main rules in this stage:

1. Try to identify best practices that would require less change for the sales representative. Usually, we looked at ways a sales person could do something they already do, better or more consistently.

2. Ensure that any expectation or activity required of the sales people was incorporated in a manner that supported the overarching organizational strategy.

3. Sales people had to be actively involved in this stage, and we needed to utilize data collected from different customers.

Once we knew what needed to change, we helped the organization develop new measurement systems and reward structures to encourage adoption of the new expectations and create real accountability among sales people.

We also first focused our efforts on management, helping them understand personal change and how to coach people through such an effort. Then we incorporated training customized to create an emphasis on this company's issues. The most important aspect of the entire effort was the philosophy we utilized:

How can we influence our customers in a way that builds more trust in our relationship and promotes success for them?

Again, trust and success are two fundamental ingredients in these efforts. It is important to remember, that we were not identifying influencing tactics that would promote sales success. We were promoting their customer's success. Sales people's success is a by-product of customer success.

It is important to note that, while sales people were worried about how this change effort would affect their ability to meet their goals and many of them felt it difficult to temper their agendas, they were successful. They were successful because we took a holistic approach that was truly customer-centric. In fact, this organization realized:

- A 25 percent increase in revenue generation;
- A 20 percent shift in profitability;
- Over 100 percent shift in new customers; and
- Over 25 percent shift to the positive in customer retention.

The work at this organization is not finished, by any means. They will need to continue to cement the changes, review expectations to determine whether they are still relevant, reinforce the training and customer philosophy, and maintain accountability.

Service

Companies with service approaches that recognize that customer service really is about partnering and not parroting understand the difference between solving problems and documenting problems. Unfortunately, service is often lacking more than ever. Most people are tired of automated menu options that are designed to make it difficult to speak to a human being and, if we do, the conversation is so incredibly scripted that we might as well have stayed with the automated options.

There are organizations that have multiple tiers for service. I realize they are built this way for efficiency, but for whose efficiency—the customer's or the service department's? The irony is that the first tier can rarely solve a customer's problem, so as a customer you feel frustrated for wasting time trying to solve the problem with someone who is not equipped to help you. Then you are routed, usually via email or through some system, to an advanced or senior support person who is smart and gives you a good answer—but to a different problem. Why does this happen? It happens because these senior support people have so many problems that they do not even talk with you; instead they quickly review the documentation and think they know the answer. If that does not work, you are then relegated to another department that is really a black hole for requests, and you are never given a name, just a generic email address to which to send your information. Does it sound like I have experienced this type of service? Unfortunately, I am not alone.

Solving customer problems is about being perceptive, personable, and curious. It requires questions and understanding. Service means that you as a customer service person cannot control the conversation, only facilitate it. Unfortunately, many organizations have built these departments, or at least a philosophy, based on what they believe is best for their company rather than what is best for the actual customer. Whether you are working with a bank, a hotel, a retail store, a web-hosting company, or a telephone company, the service levels and problem resolution should be all about the customer, but unfortunately, these experiences tend to be about the service representative/employee or the organization. Why does the customer come out last so often?

We are currently helping a client through such as change. They have seen, over the years, arbitrary rules and processes put into place, all with the best intentions. When they measure whether processes and standards are utilized, they score well. Conversely, when they measure problem resolution, they have seen a different story. With all of the standards and processes followed, many customer concerns are never truly resolved. For years, they measured customer service in a way that made it look like they were excelling at it. In fact, they thought their service out-stripped the competition, until they looked at service from the customers' point of view. It was at that point that they decided they had to actually teach their people to be more curious and intuitive with customers.

It was even more spectacular was watching the employees become excited by the notion that they were being entrusted with the customer relationship. These employees wanted every customer to feel appreciated and valued. They bought in very quickly to the new customer philosophy and felt closer to their organization as a result. Employee engagement is directly related to the customer experience. Employees who are engaged treat each other better and in turn the customer, as well—as long as they are allowed to.

Challenges of a Distributed Workforce

One of our other clients had a major challenge . . . they had several hundred locations and they wanted to have a consistent culture across all of them. Specifically, they wanted to have a service-based engagement culture at each location. Some of the challenges they faced included:

- The inability to fly each of their managers to a specific location for training.
- Complexity and practicality. If these managers had a difficult time using the training and did not have practical results, they would not continue to use the process.
- Time was a key issue. Managers needed to be around and available. Any training effort that removed them from the employees and customers for an extended period of time would not be feasible.
- Collaboration and sharing were very important. While much of the training delivered to these locations was delivered via technology, that might actually prove counterproductive in this case. They needed more interaction among the members of the management team, between the management team and employees, and among the employees themselves, not less.

We helped them build a standalone program for management that could be completed at each location over a year's time, during existing management meetings, as an intact management team. Each member of the management team could facilitate a meeting while the others participated. The meetings were to occur during regularly scheduled monthly management meetings with a simple and practical assignment between each meeting. The process took leadership through twelve components of an engaged service-minded culture.

The next step was to create more trust and dialogue between managers and employees. So we asked the question, "Why not teach the employees the same things, but relate the principles to their job and work?" To accomplish this, we built a set of activities that managers could perform quickly with their employees.

We utilized their daily meetings as the vehicle for the training. The meeting agenda included:

- *Past Performance:* Reviewing their numbers and goals.
- *Present Happenings:* Discussing key events, items, and issues that were currently occurring or going to happen that day.
- *Engagement Service Theme:* Culture-building activity and a call to action.

The activities followed the same curriculum the managers were going through, so it gave the employees and the managers a connection. By using brief activities to promote service, collaboration, and engagement principles, our client was able to promote a powerful culture. The key was to make the activities easy to facilitate, limit any need to prepare, and create a simple system that could be utilized on a regular basis. To accomplish these criteria, we categorized and color-coded the activities by engagement principle, and then by the type of activity—discussion, training, shift topic. Facilitator instructions for each activity were structured the same way:

- Purpose
- Time requirement
- Materials needed
- Directions
- Key questions
- Key points
- Tips, examples, and variations

The client saw significant changes in all of the locations using the process. Here are some of the results at various locations:

- A 22 percent increase in service scores;
- A 21 percent increase in target customer business;

- A 73 percent shift on a key quality service measure;
- A 9 percent increase in the number of customers; and
- A 9 percent increase in revenue.

All of these shifts occurred within a three-month period. It is amazing what can happen when you focus on more than just service. Creating more dialogue and real culture around engagement can make a significant difference to your customers and to your employees.

Questions to Ask Yourself

- What percentage of the time is your company viewed as a vendor versus a strategic partner?
- How much collaboration is taking place with your customers?
- To what degree are you bringing added value to your client relationships?
- How has your company defined loyalty? How should it define loyalty?
- How do you create trust in the sales process and customer relationships?
- To what extent are your sales people directly interested in the success of your clients? How is that interest demonstrated?
- How would you define your organization's service philosophy?
- Have you overused process, standards, or technology in your service efforts? Think about this from your customer's point of view.
- How have you encouraged intuition, curiosity, and collaborative problem solving in your service efforts?

- To what extent do you have a shared culture across multiple locations?
- How have you reinforced service and engagement in the daily lives of your distributed employees?
- How have you created more dialogue between management and employees in various locations?

12

REAPING THE REWARDS

In This Chapter

▶ Four Levels of Engagement

▶ Engagement in Difficult Economies

▶ A New Definition of Engagement

▶ Impact of Engagement

"Winner takes all" is a phrase that has been used in movies, books, and around card tables. In today's world, the "pie" or market share is divided up with added pressure and competition. It will become increasingly difficult to gain or keep market share without an advantage. Your people are your advantage. Your employees drive your success. It is either that, or it is the opposite. Your people become your disadvantage. Your employees hinder your success.

If you think about anything that happens in your organization, it happens through and because of people. Innovation, problem solving, decision making, execution, process improvements, customer service, sales, research and development, and the list goes on. If people are curious, hold trust in each other, are perceptive and accountable, and can concentrate on the customer, you will increase your chance of winning significantly. If, on the other hand, your employees are focused on themselves and their concerns, lack trust in the organization, lack

Figure 12.1 Four Levels of Engagement

Level 1	Employee Engagement is **Ignored**
Level 2	Employee Engagement is an **Event**
Level 3	Employee Engagement is a **Process**
Level 4	Employee Engagement is a **Strategy**

Source: Performancepoint, LLC

ownership, and concentrate on making management happy because they are afraid, you will surely fall backward. In today's world of winner-takes-all stakes, why would you not try to create this advantage?

As organizations grow and mature, so do silos, as different functions build their own power bases and so there tends to be less collaboration, rather than more. Using the engagement drivers discussed earlier in this book to promote more trust and achievement, you can help bring it all together. Push yourself and your organization to learn more about this subject and to approach engagement more holistically and systemically. One way to measure your organization's current state and progress with employee engagement is to use the four levels of engagement seen in Figure 12.1.

Four Levels of Engagement

Level 1: Employee Engagement Is Ignored

Many organizations do not pay attention to employee engagement. These organizations simply ignore it altogether. In fact, only 27 percent of organizations have a formal engagement process and 19 percent do not have it on radar at all.[1] This is, of course, an easier road to travel in some ways. Organizations that do not focus on engagement have less to measure, less to think about, less to change, and set little to no expectations with their associates. It can feel better to ignore employee engagement because if you are not looking critically at your organization, and possibly yourself and your team, you can convince yourself that all is well in the world—that your employees are leaving because of compensation issues rather than leadership issues, that policies instead of a more productive culture will solve your challenges, and that poor performance is just the result of a new generation's lack of work ethic rather than the organization's career development process. The bigger question is: "Where could we be as an organization if we did focus on engagement?" We know from research that disengaged employees in the United States alone cost our businesses between $270 billion and $343 billion annually and we also know that 73 percent of businesses that have started employee engagement programs have increased their operating profits.[2] With numbers like that, ignoring employee engagement seems crazy. The challenge in these organizations usually rests with the leadership. Some leaders see the employees as the problem. They will cite work ethic issues, attitude problems, and a host of other reasons why they struggle in getting employees to be more productive or to stay longer. Some leaders hold out the organizational results as if it were a carrot. I had one CEO say, "I work on those issues when they bring in more money." This mindset is completely backwards. Leaders should be asking, "Why are we having these issues?" or "What are we doing as an organization that is hindering our people's ability to engage?" One last question these leaders should ask themselves is, "What if . . .?"

Level 2: Employee Engagement Is an Event

The second level is viewing engagement as an event. Typically, this is triggered by a change in the organization such as a new president or a request by someone in the organization, or because an organization has come out of difficult times and wants to do a survey because it seems safer now to make the effort. The trouble with this approach is that it typically lacks a champion and a reason to keep going. Because the original exertion was situational, the future of the event will most likely diminish. This can be even more damaging than ignoring engagement altogether, since expectations are raised when an organization starts such an effort. Starting an engagement effort, especially a survey, is not an objective event, and employees watch to see what changes will occur. If an engagement effort is short-lived, employees tend to believe the organization does not care about them. In some cases, outright backlash and animosity will occur. Starting and stopping engagement efforts will lead, at the very least, to reduced trust, and possibly a complete breakdown and increased turnover, and in some cases employee sabotage.

Another problem with this approach is the underlying message we send. Our employees see the event in subjective terms. The event becomes a vehicle that sends this type of messages:

- Leadership wants to gain information that demonstrates a positive environment.
- They want to look good in front of the board.
- Engagement only counts when it is easy.
- They only care when they think we will walk out the door.

The challenge relates to *trust*. Trust is developed by behaving consistently. If we pay attention to employee engagement inconsistently, then we are only decreasing engagement over time. We must remember that there are rarely good or bad times to have an engagement process. There is really no such thing as good news or bad. The results of a survey, program, or a process are just that—results. What you choose to do with those results will determine your progress.

Level 3: Employee Engagement Is a Process

The third level of organizational engagement is treating engagement as a process. This seems realistic and proper at first glance, and it represents a significant improvement over the first two levels. Organizations that treat engagement as a process typically see engagement as a "people" effort, and the champion of the effort is human resources or a subset thereof. In fact, 40 percent of organizations that have a formal process utilize human resources to house their employee engagement programs.[3] Usually these efforts are completed on a shoestring budget, and the emphasis lies with collecting the data and showing an improvement in the rating year over year. The challenge here is that there is no shared ownership across the organization; the engagement effort is barely on top management's radar; the effort usually does not account for real impact; and the organization is cost-conscious. This causes the data collection/analysis to be sloppy, results in little to no wisdom, and at its worst to be completed in-house, which causes a lack of perceived and possibly real confidentiality.

Another issue with treating employee engagement as a process is that it is typically perceived as an employee satisfaction effort and is treated as such. Forty-four percent of those organizations that measure employee engagement utilize a standard opinion or satisfaction survey and only 23 percent utilize an employee engagement survey.[4] Most of the time, there is a perception that there is little difference between the two options, but there is a vast difference between surveys and programs. Employee engagement efforts are built on more recent and relevant research that takes into account the current workplace and economic environment.

Level 4: Employee Engagement Is a Strategy

The fourth level is engagement as a part of an organization's strategy. This assumes that either the organization has indirectly or directly made the connection between engagement and the success measures for the organization. When an organization sees engagement as central to its success, the entire process is treated extremely differently. First, senior management is heavily involved in the engagement effort, from debriefings on surveys to sponsoring engagement action plans. Another shift that occurs is that engagement issues are discussed at the executive levels of the organization. In organizations that treat engagement strategically, engagement is discussed regularly, on equal footing with marketing, finance, and operations. Organizations at this level typically measure engagement, monthly or quarterly in some way, on top of an annual survey. Rather than seeing the measurement as a number that must always be bested, the organization sees the measurement results as an indicator as to whether progress has been made. The last difference at this level is the number of and types of communication regarding engagement efforts. There is more communication, it is more candid, and it is provided through more communication vehicles. These organizations also garner stronger results than their competition, financial and otherwise, and build a brand along the way.

There are times, especially during difficult or challenging economies, that organizations pull back from these efforts. I say it is the wrong thing to do. Think about how a recession affects people. They become fearful and self-oriented and begin to not only lower their expectations, but also to waste time. People respond in a manner opposite to what they should. In an effort to protect themselves, they typically do themselves and their organizations harm. One survey found that, during a recession, employees wasted more of their day than in a normal economy. In fact, time wasting increased by 44 percent. Most of the top time-wasting activities during a recession demonstrate the fear and self-interest that people have during bad times:

- Using the Internet to look for better employment;
- Using the Internet regarding money and finances; and
- Worrying or thinking about negative subjects.[5]

These are the reasons why we lose ground during these times. A recession is difficult, but it is also a time when the deck of cards gets reshuffled. Some organizations land on top and others land on the bottom. Some organizations gain market share, while others lose it. And the biggest myth is that all organizations do poorly. Some companies have double-digit growth in profit and revenue when their competitors are falling apart. Why? Because they stay focused on what matters and they deal constructively with their most important asset . . . their employees.

Engagement in Difficult Economies

During bad economic times, we must take extra precautions. We must help our employees lead us out of darkness because they are the path to success. Specifically, during bad economic times we should:

Focus on Transparency

It is way too easy to hold back information, opinions, or issues as a way to protect your employees. It is hard to openly put it out there and discuss the issues. However, when we do not discuss the "truth" of what is happening, we do not give permission to our employees to discuss what is on their minds. Our employees then turn to gossip, negative thoughts, and time-wasting activities rather than productive efforts.

Focus on Senior Leadership Efforts

Senior leadership needs to communicate more in difficult moments. Face-to-face is best when possible. Share the strategy for getting through the tough times and how you can use this difficult phase to better set the company for success when times turn around. Allow employees to question the strategy. A great number of people become comfortable with an idea or learn about an idea from questioning.

Focus on Consistency

Do not stop your engagement efforts. Keep surveying your employees. Continue with your action planning; appreciative inquiry, and other efforts to support the engagement process. Your organization may need to narrow the focus on its efforts or phase your efforts in over time, but progress will send the right message to your employees. Spend more time analyzing the data to focus your efforts on the most important and impactful opportunities.

Focus on Celebrating

Find your successes with engagement efforts and in general. People need to find things to feel good about during difficult economic times. When something like gaining a new client occurs during a challenging economic period, take a moment, feel good, and thank those who made it happen. Pause. Then look to see how you can repeat it.

Focus on the Customer

Don't pressure your people about revenue and profit. That is weight a leader must bear. We should not scare our people into success because we are worried. Be honest and authentic, but, most of all, help everyone get back to the basics. Remember what made your business special in the first place. Remember why customers saw value in your products and services. Help your people put your customers first and out-service your competitors. Be an Engager . . . Be a Trusted Advisor. After all, it is about connections.

A New Definition of Engagement

Now that we have covered a lot of ground, let's take that definition we started with, the core definition on engagement and add to it. Let's make it even more clear and full of strength. Let's make it a definition that stands up during good times and bad and one that we strive to live by each day.

> The **degree** *to which people* **commit** *to an organization and the* **impact** *that commitment has on how profoundly they* **perform** *and their length of* **tenure**.

Three central aspects of high employee engagement levels are

- *Clearer Connections:* Individuals fortify commitment based on increasing the number and strength of the connections or mutually beneficial bonds with their work and environment.
- *Improved Trust:* Employees are able to be more present and focus on the needs of others, causing them to build high-trust relationships with internal and external customers.
- *Increased Resourcefulness:* Employees are able to see opportunities, as opposed to just managing risks, causing them to drive themselves and the business forward as they feel a sense of ownership.

When we try to live up to a workplace that allows this definition to come to life, there really is not much we can't accomplish. Our people will be passionate and successful as will our business.

Impact of Engagement

Over the last few years, we have been lucky to work with a number of great clients of all different shapes and sizes. While they are all special in some way, one in particular demonstrates how powerful employee engagement efforts can be. This client is not large, by any means, with approximately four hundred people, but they have been through a great deal. This organization,

Figure 12.2 One Client's Results

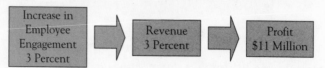

Source: Performancepoint, LLC

like so many others, has seen significant shifts in their industry; they have been impacted by a number of factors, including the economy, new leadership, and growing pains. They decided that engagement was important and that they needed to invest more energy into engaging their employees. See Figure 12.2 for their results.

We worked with this organization not just on measurement and analysis, but on action plans and creating stronger communication. This organization took the results, and more importantly the journey, very seriously. After a year, they were able to improve their engagement by 3 percent, leading to a 3 percent increase in revenue and an $11 million positive shift to their bottom line. It does not take much of a shift to create noteworthy results, and you do not have to be a Goliath to benefit, but the benefits can help you become a giant if you want to be. Most importantly, the road to wherever you are going as an organization can be more fun, more interesting, and healthier for you and your employees.

May the road ahead be well-paved and the waters you sail be calm. If they are not, listen carefully, trust your employees, and hope that you have engaged them well, because they can get you through any storm.

Notes

Chapter 1

1. BlessingWhite. (2008, April). 2008 Employee Engagement Report.
2. Performancepoint. (2007, September). Employee Engagement Study.
3. U.S. Department of Labor. Bureau of Labor Statistics. (2008, July).
4. Performancepoint. (2008, September). State of the Union Survey.
5. Performancepoint. (2008, September). State of the Union Survey.
6. European Survey on Working Conditions. 1990–1995–2000. 2005-EU-25.
7. Friedman, T. (2006). *The world is flat*. New York: Farrar, Straus & Giroux.
8. Ali, A., & Al-Kazemi, A. (2007). Islamic work ethic in Kuwait. *Cross-Cultural: An International Journal*, 14(2), 93–104.
9. Wiseman, Robert. (2008, May 11). Being a CEO has its perks, but tenure isn't one of them. *The Boston Globe*.
10. 2008 CEO turnover rate ahead of 2007. (2008, May 6). *Baltimore Business Journal*.
11. www.npr.org/templates/story/story.php?storyId=95038679. (2008, December 17).

12. Schubert, S., & Miller, C. (2008, December 21). Where bribery was just a line item. *The New York Times*, p. 1, Sunday Business.

13. http://abcnews.go.com/Blotter/WallStreet/story? id=6040990 &page=1. (2008, October 15).

14. Clements, A. (2007, April). *Human Resources* workplace stress survey 2007. *Human Resources*, pp. 29–32.

15. Presser, H. (2003). *Working in a 24/7 economy: Challenges for American families*. New York: Russell Sage Foundation.

16. Howe, J. (2008). *CrowdSourcing*. New York: Crown Business.

17. Gonzalez, V., & Mark, G. (2004, April 24–29). *Constant, constant, multi-tasking craziness: Managing multiple working spheres*. Vienna, Austria: CHI 2004.

18. Improve your attention span. (2008, October). www.real-simple.com/realsimple/gallery/0,21863,1842884–1,00.html. *Real Simple*.

19. 100 best companies to work for. (2006). *Fortune*.

20. U.S. Department of Labor. Bureau of Labor Statistics. (2006). [www.bls.gov/data/].

21. Performancepoint. (2008, September). State of the union survey.

22. Watson Wyatt. (2001). *Worldwide survey of more than 500 publicly traded companies*. Washington, DC: Watson Wyatt.

23. Wellbourne, T., & Andrews, A. (1996). Predicting performance of initial public offering firms: Should HRM be in the equation? *Academy of Management Journal, 39*, 901–911.

24. http://en.wikipedia.org/wiki/Commitment. (2008).

25. http://www.yourdictionary.com/connection. (2008).

Chapter 2

1. www.yourdictionary.com/culture. (2008).

2. http://en.wikipedia.org/wiki/Culture. (2008).

3. Roberts, B. (2008, December). How to marshal wikis. *HR Magazine*, pp. 54–57.

4. Chopra, A. (1999). *Managing the people side of innovation.* West Hartford, CT: Kumarian Press.
5. Miller, L. (2001). Take steps to combat lost institutional memory. *HR Magazine, 46*(2).

Chapter 3

1. Bolman, L., & Deal, T. (1991). *Reframing organizations.* San Francisco: Jossey-Bass.

Chapter 5

1. Dillon, S. (2008, June 15). Messages of exhortation, counsel and congratulation. *The New York Times,* p. 16.
2. Taylor, J. (2008). *My stroke of insight.* New York: Viking.
3. Dillon, S. (2008, June 15). Messages of exhortation, counsel and congratulation. *The New York Times,* p. 16.

Chapter 6

1. Branham, L. (2005). *The 7 hidden reasons employees leave.* New York: AMACOM.
2. Get real: Honest job previews can cut employee turnover. (2006). http://knowledge.wpcarey.asu.edu/article.cfm? articleid=1276. Tempe, AZ: Knowledge@W.P. Carey.
3. Corporate Leadership Council. (2004, November). *Driving performance and retention through employee engagement.* Washington, DC: Corporate Leadership Council, a division of The Conference Executive Board Company.

Chapter 7

1. Watson Wyatt. (2007). *Work USA survey, 2006–2007.* Washington, DC: Watson Wyatt.
2. www.wordcentral.com/cgi-bin/student?book=Student&va= Reciprocity. (2008).

Chapter 8

1. LaMantia, J., & Buzzota, V. (2007, April). Shut up and listen! www.linkageinc.com/company/news_events/link_learn_enewsletter/archive/2007/04_07_Listen.aspx.
2. Performancepoint. (2006, September). Employee Engagement Study.
3. Performancepoint. (2008, September). State of the Union Survey.

Chapter 9

1. *Webster's New Dictionary* (2nd ed.). (1982). New York: Simon and Schuster.
2. Smart, B. (1999). *Topgrading*. Englewood Cliffs, NJ: Prentice Hall.
3. Branham, L. (2005). *The 7 hidden reasons employees leave.* New York: AMACOM.
4. http://en.wikipedia.org/wiki/Roundabout. (2008).

Chapter 10

1. www.msnbc.msn.com/id/29033134/. (2009.)
2. www.cnn.com/2004/ALLPOLITICS/06/25/cheney.leahy/. (2008).
3. http://blogs.kansas.com/weblog/2007/06/bush_cheney_swe/. (2008).

Chapter 11

1. Sturman, M., & Way, S. (2008). Questioning conventional wisdom. *Cornell Hospitality Report, 8*(6).
2. Headd, B. (2003). Redefining business success: Distinguishing between closure and failure. *Small Business Economics, 21*, 51–61.

Chapter 12

1. www.melcrum.com/offer/etee/surveysummary.pdf. (2008).
2. www.ceridian.com/myceridian/article/1,2481,14785–65859,00
.html. (2007).
3. www.melcrum.com/offer/etee/surveysummary.pdf. (2008).
4. www.melcrum.com/offer/etee/surveysummary.pdf. (2008).
5. www.leadershipiq.com/index.php/news-a-research-/recent-
studies/143-leadership-iq-study-recession-rumination-kills-
productivity-

Index

Page references followed by *fig* indicate illustrated figure; followed by *t* indicate a table; followed by *e* indicate exhibits.

A

Accountability: commitment element of, 24; employee engagement as requiring, 28; MPV (my professional value), 187, 202–203; on-boarding process, 127; sales group, 211; victim mentality vs. engaged, 189–191. *See also* Personal responsibilities

Acknowledgement of employees, 45

Action Planning Chart, 74 *fig*

Action planning meeting: description and objectives of, 72–73; engagement conversation agenda for, 73; tips for celebrating successes, 74–75; tips for communicating results, 75–76; tips for creating successful engagement conversations for, 73–74; tips for identifying success, 75. *See also* Engagement conversations

Agendas: as connection barrier, 87–89; for engagement conversation meetings, 70–71, 73

Anxiety: employees and increasing, 9–12; macro shifts in employment environment, 6 *fig*; security and trust issues of, 10. *See also* Fear

Appreciative inquiry, 161–162

Assessment centers, 130

B

Behavior: fear impact on, 93; fears affecting new leader, 174–179; trust developed through consistent leadership, 224

Behavior-based interviewing, 116–117, 131–132

Biased research, 36–37

Bolman, L., 55

Business acumen skills, 159–163

Business structures/systems: assessing organization, 52 *e*; communication, 40–41; customer/business cycles, 45–47; incentives and acknowledgement, 44–45; innovation, 42; priority setting, 40; success indicators, 38–39; talent acquisition, 42–43; talent enhancement, 43–44. *See also* Organizational culture; Organizations

C

Candidates. *See* Job candidates

Career transitions: description and process of, 166–168; individual contributions to, 167*t*

Celebrating: engagement in difficult economies by focus on, 228; successful action planning meeting, 74–75; successful engagement conversations, 74–75

CEOs: engagement strategies during difficult economies, 227; engaging leader development role by, 153–154; executive pay debate and, 10–11; high rates of turnover by, 10; top down engagement conversations from the, 69–72 *fig*. *See also* Leadership

Change-resilience competency, 193*e*, 197–198

Cheney, D., 194

Collaboration: awareness vs. adoption of, 152; co-discovery process of, 158; between different workforce locations, 216; exemptions to promotion of, 153–154; on-the-job training for, 152–153; study findings on leadership, 150–152; technical route to, 154–155

Command-and-control organization, 96

Commitment: set of connections basis of, 24, 26 *fig*–28; Wikipedia definition of, 24

Communication: of engagement conversation results, 75–76; engagement conversation/action planning agendas, 69–72 *fig*, 73–74; lacking dexterity skills of, 171–172; open-ended questions used for, 87; reducing "noise" by improving internal, 98–99; "tabletop" discussions, 84

Communication systems: anxiety increased due to poor, 11; assessing organization's, 41–42; as engagement driver, 40–41; technology used for, 41. *See also* Feedback

Compensation: assessment of organization, 46; as engagement driver, 44–45

Competencies: new leader, 180 *t*; personal engagement, 193 *e*–200

Conference Board, 21

Confidant leadership readiness, 184 *fig*, 185

Conflict: fear component of, 80–81, 90–95; self-interest role in, 80, 82, 173–174; trust as issue in, 79–83

About the Author

Brad Federman is the president of Performancepoint, LLC, a client-driven management consulting firm specializing in employee engagement. Having spent over eighteen years focusing on the human impact in organizations, Federman has become a recognized leader in the corporate world and the performance improvement industry. He has traveled the globe consulting in North America, Asia, Europe, and the Middle East working with organizations of various industries and types. Federman has spoken at international conferences such as the American Society for Training and Development and has been quoted in publications such as *Fortune Small Business*, *HR Magazine*, and *The Los Angeles Times*.